GOSPEL
GRIT

What Jesus Showed Us and Told Us
While Backpacking Homeless

Dr. Randy R. Butler

Deep River
B O O K S

Gospel Grit
© 2013 Dr. Randy R. Butler

Published by
Deep River Books
Sisters, Oregon
www.deepriverbooks.com

ISBN – 13: 9781937756970
ISBN – 10: 1937756971

Library of Congress: 2013948375

Printed in the USA

Cover design by Jeff Miller

Special Dedication

I want to honor a friend I have known since high school. John Breitmeier and I began a friendship when we were in youth group together at Lentz Evangelical Church in Portland, Oregon, that has lasted to this day.

John is a pastor in Albany, Oregon, a thirty-minute drive from where I pastor in Salem. He suffers from a severe case of Parkinson's disease. My desire is to honor him and to bring a greater awareness to this awful disease that affects so many.

Ten years ago, after the death of my son, Kevin, John called to ask if I would go with him to a seminary class in Portland to listen to a man by the name of Randy Alcorn, who was teaching a class on the subject of heaven. John thought it might help me in my time of deep grief. He was right.

Alcorn was kind enough to interact with me and later allow me to be a small part of his world. The path I was sent on—which was nothing short of an eternal perspective mindset—changed my life. I went back to school, started writing books, taught a few classes at the college level, and learned to live with a new normal. All of this I owe initially to my friend John.

Although John suffers greatly from Parkinson's and so must restrict his ministry, he remains the senior pastor at his church. Please consider contributing toward the cure for Parkinson's, and join me in prayer that one day it will be eradicated for the sake of many, including John!

DEDICATION

This book is dedicated to all those who have gone before me as disciples of Jesus Christ. I am certain most of His disciples had it rougher than I do. I am certain most were godlier than I am. I am certain most made a far greater difference in the kingdom than I. Yet we are all called to be His disciples. Our assignments are tailored to who we are and what we were created for. We were created for His purpose.

This book is dedicated to all the martyrs, who are the true heroes of the faith. What an honor it will be to meet them when I get to heaven! Their discipleship is measured not only by how they lived but how they died.

This book is dedicated to all the disciples of Jesus Christ who will read this book and are striving to be everything they can be in Christ. May God grant each reader the grace and the determination to get it right.

This book is dedicated to the generations that will follow mine should the Lord tarry. I trust they will do a better job of following Him than we have, as we often get hung up on things that really do not matter. Maybe that is true of every generation. Nonetheless, I pray God's best for their lives.

This book is dedicated to my Savior Jesus Christ, whom I love with all my heart. I owe Him my life. In membership vows and baptisms at our church, I ask this question of each member: "Do you love Jesus with all your heart?"

I can truly say that I do. This is the essence of the gospel.

I call it *Gospel Grit*.

No matter what happens today,
God loves you very much!

CONTENTS

FOREWORD

Randy Butler is a good pastor. He loves God and he loves people, in that order. He is also a practical, down-to-earth person who loves the outdoors. So this book by Randy, *Gospel Grit,* intrigued me. Somehow the image of picking up my backpack and following Jesus captures my imagination. I confess I can think of nothing better than grabbing my backpack for a hike in the beautiful Cascade Mountains near our home.

What could it have been like to quite literally follow Jesus? Whatever the disciples carried with them, it was minimal and essential as they listened to what Jesus told them and, maybe most importantly, what He showed them by what He did. So often we approach our Christian walk in a one-dimensional way: we read what Jesus said, but too often don't fully comprehend the setting of those words and what He did.

That's why I love this book. In his frank and realistic manner, Randy compels us to catch a fresh vision of what this following means. We sense what it was like to tromp through the dusty roads after Jesus. Of course the disciples needed their feet washed! While it was a symbolic gesture, no doubt it was genuinely needed. As I read through the chronological following of Jesus as told by Matthew, Mark, Luke, and John, I get a sense of dirt and leaves and crowds of needy people along with times of retreat, reflection, and prayer. *Gospel Grit* gives us a front-row view of what it must have been like to actually follow Christ. To see what He showed His disciples. To listen to what He told them.

As we follow along with the disciples, we see that Jesus shows us where to find the living water. He shows us what it means to live by the bread of life. We see how Christ brings healing and compassion to the most unlikely people. He demonstrates what it means to truly love others, to see the interruption that was most likely the real event.

Sometimes Jesus said things and told stories that were not easy to understand. This is why the point in Randy's book—to see what Jesus actually *did,* not only what He *said*—helps us understand the One we say we follow.

When you're out hiking, that backpack is pretty important. Water is necessary, along with a map or compass and some food. In late August, I slip in a few plastic bags in case we run into a patch of huckleberries. But it's also important not to overload a backpack. I remember a few hikes when I carried a lot of nonessentials. And in our following Christ, Randy reminds us that we carry things Jesus never intended us to carry. Jesus tells us that His yoke is easy; that we are not to worry about our lives; that we can trust Him, no matter what. And even though we have tribulation in this life, through Christ we will overcome. The living water Jesus gives us never fails. His words sustain us on our journey.

Gospel Grit reminds us to cultivate the simplicity of trust and obedience in our following. How often we complicate the gospel. It's time to stop and take a fresh look, along with Randy, at what Jesus showed us and told us. Be warned, however—this kind of real-life following has a cost: it costs us being in control. But the trade-off is exhilarating! We don't have to have life all figured out. Jesus continually saw the big picture and His place in it, and when we follow Him, we can do the same.

Nancie Carmichael
MA Spiritual Formation; author and speaker

INTRODUCTION

IN 2005, I WENT BACK TO SCHOOL for what I trust was the last time. Just before the Christmas break, one of the professors in my doctoral program asked us to read the Gospels during the break. I did far more than read the Gospels; I devoured them. It seemed I was possessed by the Holy Spirit as I recorded every verse I found that reflected what Jesus *showed us* and *told us*. I was struck by hearing people talk about being a disciple or a follower of Christ while their lives did not emulate what I was reading. Now, some seven years later, I have formulated my findings for those who will find this book useful.

In *Gospel Grit,* I decided to compile everything Jesus showed us and told us to give me and others a "Reader's Digest" version of what Jesus said a disciple looks like. As I wrote, I realized this book is about living strong for Jesus. It seeks to bring following Jesus into gritty reality. It is a study on what might have taken place around the campfire with Jesus after He made a comment. It is a study on what might have been discussed walking down a dust-plagued road outside of Jerusalem. It is a study on what might have been discussed after a day of boating with Jesus.

How often do we read the Gospels without thinking about their life-changing implications? This book is my attempt to walk with Jesus, talk with Jesus, ask questions of Jesus, and try to understand what He wants following Him to look like.

As I went through the Gospels, I discovered 729 statements that reflect either what Jesus showed us or what He told us. (It's possible that I've missed a few, and some may be duplicated. But this is a fairly complete collection.) As you read this book, I strongly encourage you to read each statement in its entirety, as they are extremely powerful taken as a whole.

The contents of this book, the grit which makes up the Gospels, become the foundation, the walls, the interior, the exterior, and the landscape from which we are to model our lives after Jesus Christ. The remainder of the New Testament is what goes inside the house—that which is to be in our hearts once God has transformed them.

As you read all 729 portions of Scripture, please remember the context in which Jesus is speaking. As we read His statements this way, we catch a fresh picture of an amazing Christ who calls us to see what He did, to hear what He told us.

So, let us set the stage.

As the Gospels gain speed, Jesus is thirty years old, never married, does not have a permanent address (on earth), and consequently is backpacking throughout Israel, homeless and unemployed—while at the same time being fully God! This, truly, is an amazing story. Further, He is gaining followers by the dozens, if not hundreds, on a daily basis.

Jesus is not only gaining followers, He is making enemies—so much so that they plot to kill Him. The only reason His enemies do not kill Him sooner is that they fear the crowds that are following Jesus.

Picture with me a thirty-year-old carpenter who changed careers to a job that paid nothing for the last three years of His life, dodging in and out of crowds teaching, preaching, healing, and helping people, while at the same time relying on twelve guys to carefully watch what He showed them and carefully listen to what He told them so they would be able years later to remember those special three years and accurately write down their memories with specificity. And so they did.

Under the direction of the Holy Spirit, those first disciples gave us 729 statements of what Jesus showed them and told them. Each deserves attention. In the pages that follow, I take a brief look at all 729, with a challenge to follow each passage. Each will have either an "S" or a "T" beside it to denote "showed" or "told." In 302 passages, Jesus showed us what to do, and in 427 passages, He told us what to do. Together they make for a complete picture of how to be a follower of Jesus Christ.

There are many observations and things we can glean from this compilation. You will see repetition, parallels, commands, compassion, strong emotions, and many other things. The point is to make observations, accurately make interpretations, and conclude with applications for your own life.

My goal in life is to get to heaven. Theologically you may not care for how I state that; nonetheless, that is my goal. Everything I do is touched by that goal. However, it is not enough. I also want to make sure that what I do this side of heaven is my best for God. I want to follow Him as best I can.

Listed at the end of each section are the actual references which you can use for your own personal study. I suggest you get a notebook and journal and take time to consider: "How can I be a more fully devoted follower of Jesus?"

GOSPEL GRIT
Matthew

YOU ARE ABOUT TO EMBARK ON A JOURNEY with Jesus that will transform your life. I guarantee it! Jesus has transformed my life, and He will transform yours. The journey requires leaving behind the status quo. I am asking you to trade in the keys to your car, strap on a backpack, and spend three incredible years with Jesus.

I will break you in slowly. I will mention your backpack from time to time. By the time you get to the Gospel of Mark, you will be dealing constantly with your backpack and will discover many things about your life as you travel with Jesus.

Every follower of Jesus Christ has a backpack—we're all carrying things with us through life. Some are good, some are bad. As you read the pages of this book you will discover what belongs in your backpack and what doesn't. You will discover that some things simply are not necessary if you are going to really follow Jesus.

It turns out that Jesus has a backpack too, and you will discover the purpose for it as you read. You will discover there are items in your backpack that belong in His, and the only way to transfer those items is to follow Him. There are no shortcuts on this trip. In fact, the journey demands a minimum of three years. From there, you are likely to follow Him the rest of your life in a totally different way from a totally different perspective. I am excited for you. List your car on Craigslist or sell it to a friend or put it in a friend's garage. You will only need a backpack and a good pair of shoes and a willing heart to follow Jesus.

Ready? Let's go.

T—MATTHEW 3:15: "FULFILL ALL RIGHTEOUSNESS."

There's nothing like starting the Gospels off with a doozy (slang for something that is seemingly impossible). Following Jesus is not for the fainthearted. Nor is following Jesus for people who only have time for an hour on Sunday—unless of course the weather is nice, or there is a game on television, or the infamous Sunday-morning tummy ache arises, or...!

We learn early on in the Gospels that Jesus is not calling us to a hobby. Jesus was and still is calling His followers to a life laced with destiny, filled with purpose, and defined by meaning that comes not from religion but from a relationship with Jesus Himself.

If we are to take following Jesus seriously, we may need to rearrange our lives to fit the Gospels rather than rearranging the Gospels to fit our lives.

Asking human beings to "fulfill all righteousness" is like asking a ten-year-old to drive a car. While it sounds fun and exciting, it's not practical. What then can Jesus be talking about? Could it be He is asking us to shift our focus from ourselves to Him? Could it be He is asking us to do something that is bigger than we are? I think so. Jesus appears to be asking us to complete something that is incomplete in our lives. He is asking us to be thorough in our task. He is asking us not to miss anything (or anyone) in our assignment. He is asking us to do it under the banner of righteousness. He appears to be taking us from where we are to where He is, or at least to where He wants us to be.

With these words, Jesus is asking us to get in the car and do something big! But wait a minute. Maybe we have misunderstood Him. What if He is not asking us to *drive* the car, but to get into the car and let Him drive? That would change everything, wouldn't it? Could it be Jesus is asking us to get into the car, not to drive but to go for a ride with Him? I think so. This means that fulfilling all righteousness is not something we do but something He does through us. The point is, He is inviting us to go with Him on a very special journey so that together we will fulfill all righteousness.

Gospel Grit Challenge: Why do Christians have such a hard time traveling with Jesus? What part of the trip don't we like? Okay, it's time to turn in your easy chair for a backpack. There are some things that can only be learned by walking with Jesus and carrying a backpack!

S—MATTHEW 3:15: "JESUS WAS BAPTIZED."

I was baptized when I was nine years old. I still can remember the warm summer afternoon in Gladstone, Oregon, and the cold current of the Clackamas River. It is a highlight in my life that I have never forgotten, and its meaning deepens in my heart with each passing year.

As a pastor, I frequently baptize people. I suppose I have baptized hundreds over my thirty-three years of pastoral ministry. I teach people that to be baptized is a good thing because Jesus was baptized. The way I see it, anything we can do that Jesus did is a good thing. Because Jesus was baptized, we follow that model and baptize followers of Jesus Christ.

I teach and share these things during baptism services:

- Getting baptized does not save you.
- Getting baptized does not get you to heaven.
- Getting baptized does not forgive sin.
- Getting baptized is an outward expression of an inward work in our hearts by Jesus.
- Getting baptized is a great testimony to the people we know and love.
- Getting baptized is an act of obedience to God.

I am amazed that many Christians have never been baptized. Usually there is not a strong reason for it; they've just never gotten around to getting it done.

Early on as a pastor I discovered through a conversation with my wife that she had never been baptized. Imagine that, the wife of a pastor, and somehow she had slithered through the maze of requirements to be a pastor's wife (NOT!). Worse yet, she was a Baptist! A Baptist not being baptized is like a banana hanging on a tree with no peeling. Needless to say, the evening I baptized my wife, I figured I should hold her under for good measure. (I never claimed to be very smart. I proved that point yet one more time that evening.)

Want to be like Jesus? Get baptized! It matters. At this point you will probably discover your backpack has excuses in it. If we aren't willing to hand this one over to Jesus, it will be a long three years together!

Gospel Grit Challenge: If you have been baptized, share what that meant to you with someone who would benefit from your testimony. If you have not been baptized, get 'er done.

S—MATTHEW 3:16: "THE SPIRIT OF GOD DESCENDED ON JESUS."

(This is also found in Luke 3:21–23, making two references.)

Christianity desperately needs what we read of in these verses. We need the Spirit of God to descend on each one of us. Jesus was a game changer. He became a game changer because the Spirit of God descended on Him.

In the book of Acts, Jesus set the stage for us to get what He had. He promised the Spirit of God so we could be more like Him. Jesus performed miracles and helped a lot of people and changed the world. He asks us to perform miracles in His name. He asks us to help a lot of people. He is asking us to change the world!

I am not a fan of going to a store to try on clothes. Going into that little room and undressing within inches of total strangers…yikes! I don't know about you, but I undress and get dressed again with lightning speed. Yet it's important to make sure something fits. Sometimes we treat the things of God like I treat going to a store to try on clothes. We are uncomfortable with the very thought. We rush God, trying on things He wants us to wear that we think are not a good fit. Just as the Spirit of

God descending on Jesus was a good fit, so the Spirit of God is a good fit for followers of Jesus Christ. In fact, without the Holy Spirit we are like the emperor wearing his new clothes (I trust you know that story!).

Gospel Grit Challenge: What regarding the Holy Spirit descending on believers makes so many so uncomfortable? What about it makes you uncomfortable? Why do some feel that the Holy Spirit is not a good fit?

S—MATTHEW 3:17: "THIS IS MY SON WITH WHOM I AM PLEASED."

(See also Luke 3:21–23, making two references.)

I love my children. You love your children. God loves His Son. Every parent wants to be pleased with his or her child. But look closely here: as far as ministry goes, Jesus hadn't done anything yet. Yet His Father said that He was pleased with Him.

The relationship between the Father and the Son was such that the requirement for pleasing the Father was not performance, just the relationship. This is what Jesus wants us to capture in following Him. We are the children of God. Perhaps some of us struggle with performance based Christianity. Do we need to bear fruit? Yes. Yet the requirements for pleasing God are simply loving God, knowing God, obeying God, and worshiping God. These things are not a burden; they are a joy.

Jesus is showing us the importance of our relationship with the Father. We want to be pleasing to God. Yet we so often turn this into a burdensome matter of works. The smallest thing my children do pleases me. Just being with them pleases me. Think of following Jesus not so much in terms of rules that have to be followed and assignments that need to be completed. Instead, think of following Jesus in terms of just being together with Him on the trails of life and enjoying the journey.

Gospel Grit Challenge: What parts of following Jesus are hard for you? What are ways we have made following Jesus more difficult than it needs to be?

S—MATTHEW 4:1: "JESUS WAS LED BY THE SPIRIT INTO THE WILDER-
NESS TO BE TEMPTED BY THE DEVIL."

(See also Mark 1:12 and Luke 4:1–2, three references.)

There are two places I wish the Spirit of God would not lead us: the wilderness and the temptation of the devil. Of all the places and events in life, these are two I would rather skip.

I have been known to go hunting for deer and elk from time to time. I have been lost on more than one occasion. One time I got lost and night came, along with cooler temperatures. My survival skills are more like a comedy show. When I was finally found by my party, I wanted to kiss every one of their dirty, beard-filled faces for "saving my life."

On another occasion I was lost during a day that was cold, wet, and foggy. The fog was thick, the air was miserably chilling, and the rain would not stop. I am sure I provided comic relief for all the deer watching me walk through their house. I stumbled onto a road, heard a car, and went running toward the roar of his engine, firing my gun in the air to get his attention—only to discover it was the game warden! He graciously had me jump in his rig and took me all the way back to camp. Why I go out year after year to be further humiliated and tortured is one of the great mysteries of my life. On this particular day it didn't matter what was in my backpack, I was lost.

People can get lost following Jesus when they don't pay attention to where He is leading them. As we start this journey, the key is to follow Jesus closely. Remember that!

The Holy Spirit *will* lead us into the wilderness. He leads us not so that we will get lost, but so we will better recognize our need for a guide. Likewise, the Holy Spirit permits us to be tempted by the devil. (My second book, *Forecasting Temptation,* addresses the particulars of this subject.) Why does God place us in the lion's den? My best guess is that God wants us to know that we need Him. It goes to the heart of relationship. We need Him all of the time, not just some of the time. Being led by the Spirit to be tempted by the devil is God's way of saying, "Stay close to My Son." Once we have been confronted by the devil,

Jesus grabs our backpack and our hand and helps us hightail it out of trouble!

Gospel Grit Challenge: Reflect on ways you have grown closer to God when led into the wilderness. Talk about victories that were won in your life when you faced the devil and God delivered you. Share your experience with another Christian and encourage them to do the same with another.

S—MATTHEW 4:2: "HE FASTED FORTY DAYS AND FORTY NIGHTS AND BECAME HUNGRY."

(See also Matthew 6:17 and Matthew 17:21, three references.)

Fasting for forty days and forty nights is something I have never done. I love eating. My job requires eating. Yet following Jesus in this way is something I really want to do before I die. I know there is value in it, and I know I would experience a closeness to God that is like no other experience in Christianity.

What is the purpose of fasting? Why forty days and forty nights? How would I get started? Why would I do it? Is it necessary? These are all questions that have been asked of me, and honestly, questions I have asked myself.

In attempting to follow Jesus, this is a tough one. Interestingly, Scripture records only one time that Jesus fasted for this length of time. So long-term fasting is the exception, not the rule.

The purpose of fasting is obedience to God for a reason that He sometimes reveals and sometimes does not. It is all about obedience. I have no definite answer about the number forty. Then again, there are quite a few things about Christianity for which I do not have definite answers! Each time I fast, it is Spirit-inspired and directed. I do not fast just to do it. I need purpose in what I do. Once directed by the Holy Spirit to fast, I rearrange my schedule so it can be done. I share with my wife why I won't be eating dinner when I get home from work and so on and so forth. I rearrange any appointments that are scheduled around a meal and adjust. I do it because God is telling me to do it and for no other reason. If God is telling me to do it, then it must be necessary for some reason not yet revealed to me. I do, however, see definite benefits from fasting. The very least is a dependence on God and a real sense of His holy presence. I also feel closer to God after the fast is over.

So why would Jesus fast, and why should we follow His example in fasting? To get closer to the Father and to do His will. Those reasons are good enough for me. I hope they are good enough for you too.

Every time I carry my backpack, I put food in it. On this particular day with Jesus, no food is necessary!

Gospel Grit Challenge: Are you open to fasting? Talk about some potential victories that could be won through fasting that are not currently being won in your life today. Find another Christian or share your thoughts in a small group that you may be a part of.

T—MATTHEW 4:4: "IT IS WRITTEN, 'MAN SHALL NOT LIVE BY BREAD ALONE, BUT ON EVERY WORD THAT PROCEEDS OUT OF THE MOUTH OF GOD.'"

(See also Luke 4:4, two references.)

Food is often used as an analogy in the Gospels. Food is something we all need in order to survive. Jesus is teaching us several lessons in this verse.

First, He is teaching us the importance of knowing what the Bible says. Had Jesus not spent time in the temple as a boy, would He have known what the Scriptures said? I know He is God and knows all things, yet part of the reason for His being fully human is so that He can relate to us in every way (and more to the point, so that *we* can relate to Him in every way). It is about a relationship. Either way, Jesus needed to know the Scriptures when He faced the devil. We would do well to gain the same knowledge for the same reason.

Second, Jesus is teaching us the importance of living for things beyond the flesh. Hedonism, which means "if it feels good then do it," and materialism, which is the accumulation of stuff, are each geared to the flesh. They are the way of our culture. Jesus comes along and tells us to lay aside the desires of the flesh and start thinking more about the spiritual matters in life.

Third, Jesus tells us that we are to *live on* or *count on* or *rely on* what proceeds out of the mouth of God, the Bible. It is hard to rely on what we do not know, and it is hard to count on what we do not have. Jesus challenges us to live life on the spiritual plane and not the flesh-driven plane.

Further, the obvious point Jesus is making is that we need to know more of what the Bible says, not less of what the Bible says. We can infer that there is a direct correlation between how we deal with the devil and how well we know the Bible.

Ultimately, the end is not in knowing the Bible. What matters in the end is a relationship with Jesus Christ. Did you remember to pack your Bible in your backpack? There are no Gideons available on this particular trip, putting Bibles in hotel rooms to bail us out. You are going to need *your* Bible for this journey!

Gospel Grit Challenge: How can we help one another spend more time reading the Bible? And how can we be more consistent in reading the Bible? Further, how does reading the Bible translate into a stronger relationship with Jesus Christ?

T—MATTHEW 4:7: "IT IS WRITTEN, 'YOU SHALL NOT PUT THE LORD YOUR GOD TO THE TEST.'"

(Found also in Luke 4:12, two references.)

Whenever I think about school, I think about tests. Whenever I think about tests, I think about throwing up, as I was never very good at taking tests. The anxiety they caused me was painfully painful. I now teach as an adjunct at a university, and on a good day, I give my students tests that reflect grace. On a bad day I give them tests that remind me of my childhood in school!

Children are notorious for testing their parents. Now that my kids are grown, I enjoy watching other parents interact with their children. It is a blast watching parents try to smile at me when their child just put a fist through a stained-glass window at church. I love watching them balance trying to be nice in front of me while telling their child "No," when in fact we all know that if I were not around, the dust would fly and there would be dirt to pay!

Our putting God to the test is on a grander scale than children putting their parents to the test or an employee testing an employer. Jesus is telling Satan that of all the dumb things he has done to discredit God, this is among the dumbest. Jesus simply states the facts. Don't test God.

Testing God is a bit like fleecing God. I know some put out fleeces because of the example given in the Old Testament, but I would encourage people to look at the New Testament model of faith, which I believe replaces fleecing God. Over and over God tells us to put our faith in His Son, Jesus Christ. By the way, this is not just New Testament, it is Old Testament too!

I would encourage followers of Jesus to *trust* Him, not test Him. I would encourage followers of Jesus to have *faith* in Him and not fleece Him. Just because I do not understand something God is doing in my life does not mean I need to challenge Him. He cares for me, and for you. He loves us. He wants what is best for us. He will take care of us. You can count on it! These truths make it easier to stay on the dusty trail with Jesus.

Once again, it's time to look at our backpacks. Often the things we carry in there are for the times we choose not to trust Jesus. Before this trip is over, Jesus will ask you for those items. You will not need them if you follow Him closely!

Gospel Grit Challenge: What can you do to move from questioning and challenging God to fully trusting God to do things His way? How can we help one another do this?

> T—MATTHEW 4:10: "GO SATAN! FOR IT IS WRITTEN, 'YOU SHALL WORSHIP THE LORD YOUR GOD, AND SERVE HIM ONLY.'"

(See also Luke 4:8; two references.)

I am a bottom-line sort of guy. Sometimes the bottom line is a great thing. I do not need to know forty-three reasons why I need to buy a product. Just tell me how much it costs.

On one occasion, in a weak moment, I let a vacuum cleaner salesman into my house. I was actually very impressed with the product. After the sales pitch, I had to ask repeatedly how much this miracle machine from heaven was going to cost. Would you like to venture a guess? The quote that day was more than I paid for my car, more than I paid for my wedding, more than the delivery of my first child! (Besides, there isn't room for a vacuum cleaner in a backpack. In fact, there isn't room for a lot of the stuff we think it's cool to have!)

My point is, do not let Satan talk you into letting him into your house. His presentation may be impressive, but it will cost you more than you can afford!

Jesus tells us to worship God and serve God. That is our bottom line, and it is what separates us from Satan. As followers of Jesus Christ, our calling in life is to worship God and serve Him only. How do we pull this off? By being serious biblical followers of Jesus Christ. There you have it. To follow Jesus is to not follow Satan. You can only be on one trail, following one leader. Whose trail are you on?

Gospel Grit Challenge: In what ways can you multiply your worship and service to God? Consider answering in the context of following Jesus more closely. What would that look like?

> T—MATTHEW 4:17: "JESUS BEGAN TO PREACH AND SAY, "REPENT, FOR THE KINGDOM OF HEAVEN IS AT HAND."

There are many places in the Bible and specifically the Gospels where we can spend our time and attention. However, I would suggest that this singular message of repentance is at the heart of the Gospels. I understand the need to help others, and I understand the need for personal piety. But I also understand Jesus had a primary message, and this is it.

If we are going to be serious followers of Jesus Christ, it is important not to change His message for our gain, but to follow His message that others might gain! I am not certain we can change society, but we certainly can *help* society. I am not certain everything in life is *fair,* but I am certain repentance of sin will lead people to the One who is *fairest.*

Repentance is a confrontational message. It is a convicting message. Yet it is His message. If we want a different message, we need a different person to follow. I would urge us to follow Jesus Christ by first repenting of our sin and then telling others about His message of repentance. Again, it goes back to who this journey is about and who is the leader of this camping trip. In fact, it goes further than that. Jesus not only is the leader, He created the dirt we walk on. We are not asked to own the message, yet we are to recognize that we *owe* Him because of the message. There will be more on this subject throughout our journey into what Jesus showed us and told us. This verse is our starting point.

Do you remember the last time you had food poisoning? Getting the poison out one way or the other made the pain go away, and healing was on the way. So it is with repentance. It is God's way to get the poison out of us so that healing can be on the way. Hopefully you have the stomach for this angle on repentance.

Gospel Grit Challenge: Reflect on times of healing after you repented. Discuss with others why we sometimes carry sin when it only hurts us. How can we make the message of repentance more attractive through our testimony?

T—MATTHEW 4:19: "FOLLOW ME, AND I WILL MAKE YOU FISHERS OF MEN."

(See also Matthew 8:22, Matthew 9:9, Matthew 10:37, Matthew 10:38,

Matthew 16:24, Mark 1:17, Mark 1:20, Mark 2:14, Mark 8:34–35, Mark 10:21, Luke 5:27, Luke 9:23, Luke 9:59, Luke 14:26–27, John 1:43, John 8:12, John 8:31–32, John 10:27, John 12:24–26, and John 21:19—twenty-one references.)

Note above how many times in the Gospels Jesus says something to the effect of "Follow Me." We get the idea from the sheer repetition that this is pretty important stuff. We get the idea that when Jesus said, "Follow Me," He meant us to read the Bible and obey the Bible rather than debate the Bible or doubt the Bible!

Christians spend a lot of time parsing Scripture, claiming it says something other than what is literally written. I believe following Jesus is meant to be very literal and very real. For me, the question is not should I or should I not follow Christ. If we are going to be Christians, then of course we should follow Christ. For me, the questions that come to mind are things like, how often do I follow Him? How close to Him do I follow? Is there anything He did that I should not be doing? And is there anything He did *not* do that He would want me to do? I want to understand what exactly the Gospels mean to our generation, to all generations.

These questions take us far beyond what our Christian culture has done with following Jesus. We seem to stop short with wristbands asking "WWJD?" We stop short with jewelry in the image of a cross. I believe the stronger approach is to ask, "What does Jesus want us to be doing right now?" The cross I see in the Gospels is not pretty. It is not jewelry. It smells of sheep and the sulfur of hell. It is as distasteful to view as a person scarred by a life filled with destructive addictions. The cross is rugged, yet we are told by Jesus to embrace it, to pick it up and then follow Him!

As you follow Jesus, you will note that all the people around you are wearing backpacks too. The ones who are keeping up with Jesus have learned to give Him stuff from the backpack, lightening their own loads. The longer you walk with Jesus, the more you will recognize the need to give Him much of what is in your backpack, choosing to carry only the things that you truly need. It takes time, but it will happen!

"Follow Me." These may well be two of the most powerful words in the Gospels. I know this: He meant it.

Gospel Grit Challenge: What part of following Jesus is uncomfortable? What part of following Jesus is most needed in our world today? What part of following Jesus is most needed in your life today?

S—MATTHEW 4:23: "JESUS TAUGHT IN THE SYNAGOGUES, PROCLAIMING THE GOSPEL OF THE KINGDOM AND HEALING DISEASES AND SICKNESS."

(See also Matthew 8:3, Matthew 8:13, Matthew 8:15, Matthew 8:16, Matthew 9:6, Matthew 9:22, Matthew 9:29–30, Matthew 9:35, Matthew 10:8, Matthew 11:5, Matthew 12:13, Matthew 12:15, Matthew 12:22, Matthew 14:14, Matthew 14:36, Matthew 15:30, Matthew 19:2, Matthew 20:34, Matthew 21:14, Mark 1:31, Mark 1:34, Mark 1:41, Mark 1:44, Mark 2:11, Mark 3:5, Mark 3:10, Mark 5:41–42, Mark 6:5, Mark 8:23, Mark 8:25, Mark 9:27, Mark 10:52, Luke 4:39, Luke 4:40–41, Luke 5:13, Luke 5:15, Luke 5:24, Luke 6:10, Luke 6:19, Luke 7:15, Luke 7:21, Luke 8:48, Luke 8:50, Luke 9:11, Luke 9:42, Luke 13:11–12, Luke 13:13, Luke 14:4, Luke 17:14, Luke 17:17–18, Luke 17:19, Luke 18:42, Luke 22:32, John 2:23, John 4:50, John 4:54, John 5:5–6, John 5:8, John 9:1, John 9:6, and John 11:3; sixty-three references.)

Jesus healed a lot of people. We will not find a more repeated theme in the Gospels than this one. We know from reading the Gospels that Jesus exposed why He healed. It would be easy to assume healing was the priority. It was not. Jesus makes it clear that His reason for healing people was to convince the people He had the power to forgive sin. This is clearly seen in the story of the man let down through the roof in which Jesus's first concern was his soul, and He addressed the subject of sin before addressing the subject of healing.

All roads lead to the cross, not the emergency room. It might appear that Jesus is more of a doctor than a Savior. He is both. However, He healed to validate His power for what was to come on the cross. Short of the resurrection, He had no better way to show people His power to forgive sins than to make sick people well, so Jesus healed a lot of people.

Further down the road, Jesus gave instructions for His disciples to heal too. This brings up one big question in my mind: why do I not have the power or the faith or whatever it is the disciples had to heal people? I am being transparent here! But then I fall back to the reason why Jesus healed: to forgive sins. Therefore, my first priority is to proclaim Jesus. What He does with healing people is up to Him.

Does God heal today in the twenty-first century? Yes! I believe God heals in three ways:

1. Instantaneous healing, which can only be attributed to direct divine intervention.
2. Progressive healing in which prayers of healing have been prayed and then, through time, doctors, medicine, and other factors contribute to wellness. We give God glory for this type of healing.
3. Glorification is the third type of healing, which is what every Christian ultimately is promised. Glorification comes through death. This is our destiny, in which we are freed from this mortal body once and for all. It means death, which is sad for us on this side of heaven yet from an eternal perspective is the ultimate in healing.

Regardless, Jesus healed a lot of people. He has the same power to do it today. We have been given instructions in James 5 to pray for those who are sick that God might bring healing to their bodies. We must keep in mind that every sickness healed is a rainbow pointing to the power of God to forgive sins.

When I go hunting I carry in my backpack a little medical kit. Thankfully, I have never had to use it. I have it just in case I get hurt. Jesus may want that from you too one day!

Gospel Grit Challenge: Are you in need of healing? God is able! Cite instances you know of when God definitely healed someone. There may not be many. Now cite the people you know who are saved. There will be many. Salvation is healing from the penalty of sin.

T—MATTHEW 5:3: "BLESSED ARE THE POOR IN SPIRIT."

This teaching begins what is known as the Sermon on the Mount, or the three teaching chapters in the book of Matthew. Jesus teaches us many important lessons in these chapters. This line is one of the nine "blessed" teachings known as the Beatitudes. They are connected, and they are critically important to being a follower of Jesus Christ.

When my wife and I were first married, I was in seminary and we were dirt-poor compared to what we have today. We lived on about $400 a month! We never went without food, and we always had enough to pay our bills and tithe. God is faithful. Nevertheless, we did not have much. We will never forget the night we went to the shopping mall to "just look." It was dark and really wet, with rain coming down steadily as it does here in the Willamette Valley. I looked down under a streetlight, and in a puddle of water I saw a twenty-dollar bill. You would have thought we had just won the lottery.

When we recognize our spiritual poverty before God, He tells us to look under His light, and there we begin to discover the riches of His love and being in relationship with Him. This is why Jesus says we are blessed in our poverty. When we recognize who we are in light of who Christ is, it is only then that we can begin to inherit all that He has for us in this life and the life that is to come.

I invite us to neither ignore our depravity nor to boast of it, but rather to acknowledge it before God and move toward His glorious light.

Gospel Grit Challenge: Have you been able to accept your spiritual poverty in order to receive God's riches? Where do you struggle when it comes to receiving from God? Is it a deeper issue of pride?

T—MATTHEW 5:4: "BLESSED ARE THOSE WHO MOURN."

Mourning is very different from crying. To mourn is to feel within our souls a deep remorse for our sinful condition before God. It is a position that takes sin very seriously. We live in a Christian culture today that often not only shrugs sin off as no big deal, but in some circles denies that sin even exists. But to disown sin and say that it does not exist or is no big deal is to negate this teaching from Jesus. It undermines what it means to be a disciple of Jesus Christ.

Following Jesus includes letting go of what we bring to the table. We only bring it to the table so Jesus can get rid of it! Part of appreciating what Jesus has to offer is to really look at what we bring to the table. It ought to drive us to a state of deep mourning over our impoverished souls. The more colorfully we paint our souls, the more we lessen our perceived need for Jesus.

Most of us have room for growth in this teaching. I am sorry for my sin when I sin, but rarely do I mourn over it. I am wrong in my lack of mourning, yet I do not know how to practice this teaching as I think Jesus taught it.

I remember the duration of deep mourning over the loss of my son. I still mourn over it, but not like I did in the early years just after it happened. Perhaps as Christians we mourn less because with the passing of time we move further and further away from our conversion experience. While I try to forget the pain of losing a child, may God help all of us never to forget the deep, dark pit out of which Jesus pulled us.

Gospel Grit Challenge: Spend some serious time thinking about where God has brought you from. Talk about where you have come from and what God has done for you. Find some gratitude for what He has done for you and consider this teaching in light of grace.

T—MATTHEW 5:5: "BLESSED ARE THE GENTLE."

As a child, one of my favorite television programs was called *Gentle Ben*. It was about a boy and a ranger in Florida who had a black bear as a pet. At least, that is how I remember the show. I know there was a bear, and

I know it was as gentle as a pet dog.

We are not to be doormats as Christians. We are not to let the world run over us. There is a time to stand on our hind legs, growl, and let the world know we are a force to be reckoned with. Most of the time, however, we are to be as gentle as the bear I grew up watching on television. When Jesus comes into our lives, transformation takes place. The rough edges become a bit smoother. The growl becomes less intimidating. Our bite becomes less lethal, and our paws become hands of love to a hurting world.

I cannot stand fighting in relationships. I cannot stand strife. I cannot stand murmuring. All these things really wear on me emotionally and throw me out of sorts. Most Christians could stand a big dose of gentleness! If we could replace our stubbornness with gentleness, we would attract more people to Jesus.

Some people are gentle by nature. Others are not. When Jesus gets hold of us and the Holy Spirit starts walking through the rooms of our soul, the fruit of the Spirit starts to grow and blossom, and fruit is produced. A part of that fruit is gentleness. Jesus demonstrated it before Pilate and many others He could have zapped!

Somewhere early on in this journey with Jesus, we need to find room in a side compartment of our backpacks for this fruit that will begin to grow in our lives. Once you discover how good it tastes, you will not have trouble getting rid of something you once thought was so important to make room for it!

Gospel Grit Challenge: Who is the Pilate you need to be gentle before? What does God need to do in you to make room for more gentleness? It is an important part of following Jesus!

T—MATTHEW 5:6: "BLESSED ARE THOSE WHO HUNGER AND THIRST FOR RIGHTEOUSNESS."

At some time in our lives, we have all been really hungry or really thirsty or both. In fact, as I type this, I am sitting at my desk eating crackers with nothing to drink. I am going to stop right now and go get a drink of water. Oh my goodness, does water taste good when one is thirsty!

I have often been guilty of using the phrase, "I am starved." Actually, I mean that I am hungry. Most of us in the United States do not know the meaning of being hungry, not really. I have been to Haiti on seven different occasions. I love the people of Haiti. In Haiti there is hunger, real hunger. The people are not picky; they are not selective about receiving food. That is how you know you are hungry: you will eat anything. I have even seen real mud pies for sale, made of dirt and a little bit of oil to hold the dirt together.

Many Christians have become spoiled because we fail to get to a place of real hunger and thirst before God. We are feasting and filling up on things that are not good for us. We appear to be full and satisfied, when in reality our diet is like eating a bunch of marshmallows. Our stomachs are full, yet we have no real nutrition in our systems. We need to recognize that the food of God and the drink of God come from the well and plate of righteousness.

Righteousness is doing what is right in the sight of God. It was important enough for Jesus to talk a lot about it in His teaching chapters. If it is important to Him, then it needs to be important to us.

Gospel Grit Challenge: What things are you drinking and eating that are not spiritually healthy for you? Define what it means to eat and drink righteousness.

T—MATTHEW 5:7: "BLESSED ARE THE MERCIFUL."

Growing up, in school I was taught the opposite of mercy. At least, that is how I remember it. I was taught to be independent, to take care of myself, to be tough, and to be successful. I was taught that if you wanted something, you would have to work hard for it, no matter who you had to walk over. That is terrible, isn't it?

While I believe I was kind to others, I do not recall ever showing a great deal of mercy. I always thought mercy was for wimps. It turns out Jesus does not think that way at all. Jesus places a premium on mercy. He even calls the merciful "blessed."

Jesus is teaching that if we demonstrate mercy, mercy will be given back to us in exchange. In this world I have found that to be true some of the time, not all the time. But as it relates to God, it is true *all* the time, without fail.

I remember one afternoon as an eighth grader ending up on the floor in the hallway at the end of class. A boy by the name of Curtis (I would never give out his last name in case he sees this book) deliberately broke my pencil before class ended. He was bigger and stronger than I was. Most of the girls were too. Upon entrance into high school I weighed seventy-four pounds and was not much taller than five feet. (This would become the main reason why I lettered in golf in high school and not football.)

I had a choice to make: ignore Curtis and walk away, or break his pencil in return. I chose the latter. I chose poorly. The bell rang, and as we walked out into the hallway, he rang my bell. I remember lying on the floor with a bloody nose. He was mean to me all the time, and I'd had enough of him that day. That was normal in those days at school. Today they call it bullying!

Had I shown mercy and not broken his pencil, I suppose he would have left me alone. Over the course of life, following Jesus Christ includes walking away from bullies who deserve no mercy. We have much to learn from Jesus on this teaching point.

Gospel Grit Challenge: Have you ever been in a fight? How could mercy have made a difference? Ever been in an argument? How could have mercy made a positive difference? It is a part of following Jesus.

T—MATTHEW 5:8: "BLESSED ARE THE PURE IN HEART."

Our church has a group of people who are mentally impaired or physically impaired. They are God's chosen people. Every year at Christmas, we have a night where people in the church can share their talents. Clearly, this is the longest service of the year. And clearly, for many, it is the most prized of the year. Our "Pure in Heart" class usually shares three songs. It takes a bit of time to get twenty-five of them onto our platform, but it's well worth it. They sing from the depths of their hearts the songs of Christmas. Technically, they are terrible. However, to our church family, to me, and I am certain to heaven, theirs is the most prized performance of the night.

When they are finished singing, we as a congregation give them a standing ovation longer than the best singer in our church would receive in a lifetime. Why? Because each of us desires to have their heart. They have pure hearts.

If the world had their hearts, there would be no more war, no more fighting in Congress, no more divorce, no more criminals, no more jails, no more need for handcuffs or judges. If the world could embrace Jesus's teaching on the value of having a pure heart, the world would be changed forever.

If you are not mentally impaired, you are at a disadvantage. You have learned to hate, fight, and hold a grudge. Jesus could have done the same to the characters He spent time with. He chose to give them the benefit of the doubt. That is part of having a pure heart. If we want to take the teaching of Jesus seriously, we must do a better job with heart purity.

Gospel Grit Challenge: What can you identify that you can let go of so you can have a shot at a pure heart? Is it a relationship or a circumstance? Talk about it with someone.

T—MATTHEW 5:9: "BLESSED ARE THE PEACEMAKERS."

We could sure stand a dose of peacemaking in this world. While we see pockets of it from time to time, I am convinced we will not have world peace anytime soon. It seems like everyone is fighting these days. Families are fighting, married couples are fighting, churches are fighting, countries are fighting, and Congress is fighting. We just cannot seem to get this one right.

Jesus puts a priority on this teaching. Ultimately, if we are ever going to have seasons of peace, there must be peacemakers. It is going to take some courageous people to lead the way. Peacemaking is a strength, not a weakness. It is missing on every street and neighborhood in every country of the world. Nonetheless, Jesus puts it on the map for us to consider. Can we find Christians who will be peacemakers just because Jesus said to? There are a lot of backpackers out there, but not many have peacemaking in their backpack.

Peacemaking requires compromise and sacrifice; it requires giving up our need to be right. We have too many people walking around striving to be right. In their desire to be right, they create wrong. Our desire should be to be peacemakers rather than to always prove how right we are. I am not addressing tolerance or wishy-washy Christianity here. I am addressing a void. Where are the peacemakers? It was important to Jesus; it needs to be important to us.

Gospel Grit Challenge: Was there a time in your life when peacemaking would have brought about a different outcome than the one you experienced? What situation right now could be made better by being a peacemaker?

T—MATTHEW 5:10: "BLESSED ARE THOSE WHO HAVE BEEN PERSECUTED FOR THE SAKE OF RIGHTEOUSNESS."

In America, we have not yet experienced persecution. We think being teased is persecution. We think having some religious freedom taken away, such as having the Ten Commandments removed from a public corner, is persecution. Persecution, real persecution, is experienced by many Christians around the world. By all reports, it has made them and the church stronger and more effective.

Christians in America would benefit greatly from persecution. It would change our conversation. It would bring Christians together. It would make us more evangelistic, not less evangelistic. It would make us stronger, not weaker.

Jesus says in several places in the Gospels that the world is going to hate us. We have held a majority for a long time in this country. But I believe I am living in a day when we have turned the corner to being the minority. Persecution is around the next corner, and most of us are not ready for it. Our Christianity is casual and lazy. We are living not with expectation of the return of Christ, but with the expectation of our next vacation. Our minds are not really on the lost; they are elsewhere.

Being a follower of Jesus through the Gospels will either make you a stronger follower of Jesus Christ or push you to falling away from Jesus Christ. May God help each of us prepare ourselves for persecution. It is coming to a town near you!

Gospel Grit Challenge: What are you doing to prepare yourself for persecution? What are you doing to help others prepare for persecution?

T—MATTHEW 5:11: "BLESSED ARE YOU WHEN PEOPLE INSULT YOU AND PERSECUTE YOU, AND FALSELY SAY ALL KINDS OF EVIL AGAINST YOU."

(See also Matthew 5:44, Matthew 10:23, and Luke 6:35; four references.)

Easily the hardest thing for me as a pastor is dealing with the untrue and unkind words that are said about me. Because of the culture in which we live, to defend myself is to open myself up for lawsuits. Others are allowed to say whatever they want about me, yet I am not allowed in my position to tell the rest of the story. That stinks!

I have discovered that the meanest people in the world are often Christians. I wonder who Jesus was referring to when He gave us this teaching. I really am starting to think He was including mean Christians in this verse! I am not creating my own whine session here, I am simply telling you what I see and hear amongst Christians. Perhaps this resonates with you. If it does, I am sorry for the hurt that has come your way. Let me encourage you in the Lord. Stay the course in spite of people who do not know when to keep quiet.

Perhaps those in church are getting us ready for the real battle that is about to take place. In the United States of America, we are on the verge of becoming fully demonized as Christians. If we do not publicly say what is politically correct, we become a target. I believe we are in the early stages of this becoming a reality for followers of Jesus Christ in America. I wish it were not true, but what I hear and see tell me otherwise.

Gospel Grit Challenge: Have you been hurt by another from within Christianity? So has Jesus. Write that person's name on a piece of paper and burn it. Determine not to let them hurt you again.

T—MATTHEW 5:12: "REJOICE AND BE GLAD."

This is much easier said than done. This teaching was given in light of the previous teaching, which speaks of hurtful words that are likely to become glued onto our hearts. When I think of rejoicing and being glad, I think about the day a baby is born, about getting a hole-in-one on the golf course, or about bowling a perfect three hundred. When I think of rejoicing I think about an awesome dinner, Thanksgiving Day, or worshiping God on a Sunday with the rest of my church family.

But this is not the context of this teaching. Jesus is not telling us to rejoice within a happy setting. His command is within the context of duress and hurt and possible bodily harm. Jesus does not ask us to be "fair-weather Christians." He asks us to let our light shine when someone is trying to put it out. He asks us to be like Him as He was before His peers. He has promised us a great reward for this kind of behavior.

You have a choice today in how you react to life, circumstances, and relationships. You have an opportunity to let these things and people affect you adversely, or you can have an effect on them. The former will beat you up, while the latter will leave you with a great victory. If rejoicing was not the best response to life, Jesus would not be asking us to do it. Just do it!

Gospel Grit Challenge: Under what circumstances do you struggle with rejoicing and being glad?

T—MATTHEW 5:13: "YOU ARE THE SALT OF THE EARTH."

(See also Matthew 5:14, two references.)

Do you remember as a child playing the game of tag? As I recall, the goal was to touch someone else so they would be "it," whatever that means. Jesus has touched us, and we are "it." We are His ambassadors, His representatives, His hands, His feet to take His message to the world we live in.

My wife ran track in high school and college. She was really good at it. I was never remotely interested in track and field, but like a lot of other things when you get married, you learn to like things you never did before. Once in a while I will watch a track meet on television. One event I enjoy is the relay race, where the baton is passed from runner to runner. Given all the time they practice, you would think passing the baton off safely would be a cinch. But it seems like more times than it should, the baton is dropped.

Jesus is stretching out His hand to our hand as we run our race. The baton is within our reach. Once we have the baton in our hand, we become salt and light to a world that is in desperate need of Jesus Christ.

Gospel Grit Challenge: What are you doing with your baton? Any chance you can run a little faster? What will that look like? What will be different?

T—MATTHEW 5:16: "LET YOUR LIGHT SHINE BEFORE MEN IN SUCH A WAY THAT THEY MAY SEE YOUR GOOD DEEDS."

(See also Matthew 10:5, two references.)

This teaching has at least two points we cannot avoid. First, it appears the central theme of following Jesus Christ is to let our light shine, which to me says my walk with Christ is not meant to be kept a secret. Would you agree with me that there are quite a few Christians who have never come out of the closet? Would you agree with me that if Christians would switch from a 25-watt bulb to a 100-watt bulb, we could impact the world for Christ in a much more significant way? The ramifications of such thoughts are truly staggering.

Not only are we to be followers of Jesus Christ, we are to do it in a way that brings attention not to us, but to Jesus Christ. That should always be the goal of Christians: to point people to the source of our light, Jesus Christ.

As a child I sang in Sunday school, "This Little Light of Mine." One of my favorite parts as a little boy was when we got to the line, "All around the neighborhood, I'm going to let it shine," and we were allowed to get up out of our seats and start moving around the room with our fingers up in the air representing the light of Christ in our lives. As a little boy, anytime I was allowed to move around in church without getting in trouble was a good day!

There is a second teaching in this verse, and that is for our light to shine not only in the darkness but to shine through our deeds as we are intentional about helping others as a daily practice. Yes, Jesus teaches us to do good things on His behalf. That is what He did, and that is what we are to do. I would urge you to first make sure your personal light is shining brightly, and then I would challenge you to shine it through helping people. Why? Not so you can toot your own horn, but so you can honk His horn. We are never to receive glory as His followers; all the glory belongs to Him. This is the true nature of discipleship and following Jesus. It is never about us, it always about Him.

Gospel Grit Challenge: What watt is your bulb? What do you need to do to increase the wattage? Identify deeds you plan to shine your light through. Is there anything in your backpack hindering you from shin-

ing brightly? Remember, while deeds are necessary, because they are God's idea, they are not to be a point of boasting for us.

> T—MATTHEW 5:17: "DO NOT THINK THAT I CAME TO ABOLISH THE LAW OR THE PROPHETS; I DID NOT COME TO ABOLISH BUT TO FULFILL."

I am a volunteer chaplain for the Keizer Police Department in my town. I enjoy being with the police very much. I love the law. My grandpa was a cop and my dad was a reserve cop, so it is in my blood. As a little boy, I wanted to be a cop. I love catching the "bad guy." Maybe that is the dark side coming out of me that is not allowed in pastoral ministry. Either way, I love it!

I also wanted to be a lawyer when I was a little boy. I love watching *Perry Mason* at noon. It is still playing to this day at noon, probably in every state in the country. I thought it would be cool to be in a courtroom and stand before a judge and represent someone in a criminal case.

Law is not a popular word in today's culture. That does not bother me, because neither is going to the dentist and getting shot up with Novocain popular. But if I want help from the dentist, Novocain may be necessary. So far, they have not come up with a way to drill to China without shooting up our mouths first. In other words, some things about the journey with Jesus are not pleasant, simply necessary—though painful at times.

Jesus gives us some important teaching on the importance of the Law. He also includes the Prophets, because they were about as gloomy as the Law. For all the fuss over grace, Jesus wants us to know that while we are swallowing grace, He is telling us to leave room for the Law and the Prophets. Many Christians would like to eliminate the Law to fit a post-Scripture mentality. But the problem with eliminating the Law is you are telling Jesus He has no idea what He is talking about. That is a problem! Jesus not only says the Law and the Prophets are here to stay, but that He came to fulfill and elevate both. Jesus came to validate what Christians want to eliminate. If Jesus says it stays, then we need to change our attitude toward the Law and the Prophets.

It is almost as if Jesus is teaching us that to eliminate the Law is to eliminate cops because there is nothing to police. Likewise, to eliminate the Law is to eliminate Jesus because there would be no reason to die on a cross. Yikes! This teaching is yet another game changer.

Gospel Grit Challenge: What is it about laws and rules that bother you? Why do you not like being told what you can and cannot do? Do the words submission and authority have anything to do with it?

> T—MATTHEW 5:19: "WHOEVER THEN ANNULS ONE OF THE LEAST OF THESE COMMANDMENTS AND TEACHES OTHERS TO DO THE SAME, SHALL BE CALLED LEAST IN THE KINGDOM OF HEAVEN; BUT WHOEVER KEEPS AND TEACHES THEM, HE SHALL BE CALLED GREAT IN THE KINGDOM OF HEAVEN."

There are other references to keeping commandments in this Gospel, but their meanings are much different from the context of this teaching, so I will allow this one to stand on its own two feet.

This statement from Jesus teaches the importance of teaching. I am sure you can easily think of your favorite schoolteacher. Likewise, I am sure you can think of the teacher who was your least favorite as well. Who is your favorite Bible teacher? If you did not grow up in the church with teachers around you, you are at a disadvantage. My challenge for you is to find a good Bible teacher and learn everything you can to make up for lost time.

I had the privilege of having some great teachers while growing up in the church. My aunt Charlene was my seventh-grade Sunday school teacher. We met in the balcony of the church, which for a junior high boy was like telling a drunk to behave in a bar! I remember one Sunday while she had her back to us drawing something on the chalkboard that I should have been paying attention to, my friend Jimmy and I had a knife-dropping dare challenge (true story, really). We would hold our pocketknives above our heads and aim it at the other person's hand. That person had to move his hand before the knife arrived. There was one time I did not pull my hand out soon enough. The point of the knife hit a vein and blood was everywhere. Not only was my hand bleeding, but my aunt gave me a spanking before the morning was over.

However, of all the teachers I had as a boy, I most remember her lesson one day on the subject of lust. She referred to it as the four Ls. I will never forget what she said: "Look, then Long, then Linger, then Lust." I have used that my entire ministry in teaching. Her reward in heaven is going to be large for putting up with me and Jimmy, but even more for teaching the Bible faithfully. Charlene did exactly what Jesus told His disciples to do in this verse: she was a teacher of the Word to junior high boys. I didn't know it at the time, but my aunt put something in my backpack I would need for the rest of my life!

Gospel Grit Challenge: Is there anyone who has taught you whom you could contact and just tell that person "thanks" for being your teacher? Further, is there someone teaching you now whom you could encourage in the Lord and thank for his or her faithfulness to the Word? And if you are a teacher, do exactly as Jesus tells us in this teaching: keep and teach the commandments of Christ.

T: MATTHEW 5:20: "UNLESS YOUR RIGHTEOUSNESS SURPASSES THAT OF THE SCRIBES AND PHARISEES, YOU WILL NOT ENTER THE KINGDOM OF HEAVEN."

(See also Matthew 6:1; two references.)

With this statement, it appears Jesus is not trying to lower the standard so much as He is trying to teach us something about people and their appearances. Scribes and Pharisees were the religious "gurus" of their day. They knew everything there was to know about the Scriptures. The problem with them, according to Jesus—and His opinion is the only one that matters—was that they knew the Scriptures, yet they did not know Him.

Jesus is teaching us the importance of a relationship with Him over a relationship to the Scriptures. The Scriptures are critically important, but not as important as knowing, really knowing, Jesus.

Then there's the issue of appearances. We spend far too much time trying to impress those around us rather than the One who lives in our hearts! Ever try to impress someone and really blow it big-time? I remember the first communion I served as a youth pastor. It was on a Christmas Eve, and I was assisting my pastor on the platform where we served people twelve at a time at a fancy table. He had me wear a robe I had never worn before, and the sleeve was longer than I thought. On the first set of twelve people, my sleeve snagged the plate of bread and tipped the pieces into the pitcher of juice on the table. Do you know what balloon bread does when it comes into contact with liquid? It balloons! I had several options, none of which were good. If you would like to know how the rest of the evening unfolded and whether I got fired, you are welcome to e-mail me. Needless to say, I impressed very few that evening!

The truth is, though, that incidents like the above don't matter. We exist to impress Jesus Christ! The scribes and Pharisees made themselves the focus, which was their fatal error. Jesus is lobbing a slow pitch to us on this one so we do not miss the obvious. *Jesus is the focus!* Does that matter? Are you kidding me? He said eternity is at stake. I will let you figure this one out from here.

Gospel Grit Challenge: Who do you need to stop impressing? Is it possible you care far too much about your image? Discover ways to grow humility within your backpack.

T—MATTHEW 5:22: "EVERYONE WHO IS ANGRY WITH HIS BROTHER SHALL BE GUILTY BEFORE THE COURT; AND WHOEVER SAYS, 'YOU FOOL,' SHALL BE GUILTY ENOUGH TO GO INTO THE FIERY HELL."

Here, Jesus is addressing the subject of anger within the context of people. Anger affects people. We do not live in isolation on this one. Our actions speak louder than our words. Anger has never done our culture a lot of good. Anger is partly to blame for war, along with greed and stupidity and pride and poor judgment.

Counting to ten doesn't really help. Cold showers do not really help either. Long walks only give a person more time to simmer up, not simmer down. Kicking the cat doesn't help, and cussing out the dog doesn't change a thing. If you have an issue with anger, I would encourage you to ask God for divine intervention. Short of divine intervention, anger will continue to take root in your heart. The problem is not the other person; the problem is your anger.

Just as God can scour the drugs out of a drug addict, and just as God can boil the booze out of an alcoholic, so God can prune the anger out of you right down to the roots so that it will not get the best of you again.

Jesus is not emphasizing hell in this teaching, nor is He emphasizing people giving a reason to get angry. Jesus is addressing His followers personally because He knows this one can hurt *His* name if we get it wrong. So let's get this one right for *His* sake!

Gospel Grit Challenge: Is there anyone you need to apologize to? Do you need to ask God to forgive you for an unkind word or action? Is there anger in your heart? How can we help one another on this touchy subject? How many grudges are you carrying in your backpack?

T—MATTHEW 5:24: "FIRST BE RECONCILED TO YOUR BROTHER, AND THEN COME AND PRESENT YOUR OFFERING."

It really does not matter how hard we try, eventually, we are going to hurt one another's feelings. Jesus is telling us to reconcile. Sometimes we really do not feel like reconciling, but I do not see Jesus giving us an out on this one. He is abundantly clear: reconcile!

I teach that in marriage we have three incredible things going for us on the day of the wedding: love, trust, and forgiveness. In the context of marriage, once trust has been violated, it is very difficult to get back. But love and forgiveness can trump trust any day of the week. This is true of any relationship. There are people I do not fully trust because they have violated my trust in them, yet with love and forgiveness, we can still have a great relationship. I believe this is the ministry of reconciliation.

Jesus tells His followers to reconcile with others before they come offer Him something. He would rather you get it right with others than have your money. For all those who get hung up on money and Jesus and the church wanting our last dime, this teaching tells us what Jesus's highest priority is: relationships. Offerings are important, but relationships are where Jesus puts the greater weight.

Reconciling is hard. It is like having a stomachache and knowing the only solution is to get the poison out of us and the only way that is going to happen is to throw up. Nobody wants to throw up. But oh, the relief that follows. We always say to ourselves that we should have done it a lot sooner so we could have been well sooner. So it is with reconciliation: reconcile, and you will feel much better.

Gospel Grit Challenge: Do you need to throw up? You know what I mean—do you need to reconcile with anyone before reading on in this book? Get it done!

T—MATTHEW 5:25: "MAKE FRIENDS QUICKLY WITH YOUR OPPONENT AT LAW."

Allow me to contextualize this statement: If you work in a church, do not avoid the people you do not agree with. Include them on committees and boards and places where decisions are made. It is better to know their thinking behind closed doors than to have them slaughter you in front of your peers.

I remember when my grandma had a dispute with her neighbor over a fence line. My grandma had an attorney who told her she could not lose if she used the "adverse possession" rule. My grandma would have been far better off to have made friends with her opponent. Of course she lost, the attorney got paid in full, and Grandma lost a bit of property and a lot of money.

In our culture, this whole business of suing each other is totally out of control. I remember breaking my back at my grandma's because I fell off a ladder trimming some branches for her. Her insurance agent some weeks later met me at her house and offered me $250,000 to settle out of court. I neither went to court nor settled out of court. It was my fault; I had been careless. May God give us His strength to apply this teaching whenever it is needed, because this whole matter of fighting serves no godly purpose at all.

If you have a potential lawsuit in your backpack, get rid of it!

Gospel Grit Challenge: Have you ever lost a court case? Are you still bitter over the outcome? Allow today to be your day of freedom. Let it go. Let it go. Let it go.

T—MATTHEW 5:28: "EVERYONE WHO LOOKS AT A WOMAN WITH LUST FOR HER HAS ALREADY COMMITTED ADULTERY WITH HER IN HIS HEART."

As I reached this verse in the Gospels, I looked for other places where Jesus addresses lust. He addresses adultery on numerous occasions, but not lust. This passage is the only time I can find Him using the word in English.

Lust is at the top of a guy's temptation list. In *Forecasting Temptation*, I took a survey in my church and discovered what most people suspect: that lust is a huge issue for many Christians. I am perplexed as to why Jesus would not talk about it more, given how big of an issue it is not just for our time but, I am sure, for all time. There certainly are stories in the Bible that would support my statements on this subject. But the main mission of Jesus was to get to the cross and find ways to get us there with Him. This was His highest priority. Nobody else in the Bible could do this for us. But there are others who can help us with subjects like lust.

Lust is not gray at all. Lust is as black as the clothes worn by the late Johnny Cash.

I remember my days as a youth pastor in Eugene, Oregon. I had no idea how to entertain high school girls, so I took them to the mall to go shopping. One of the girls, whose name I would never mention, was staring so intently at a boy walking by that as she approached the escalator, she lost track of where she was and tumbled all the way down the stairs. I don't know if you would call her staring at that boy lust, but it sure resembled it to me! That is the problem with lust: it gets our eyes onto something we should not see and takes our eyes off someone we should see: Jesus.

Lust is one of those things that is not only in our backpack but finds ways to ooze out. We definitely need to follow Jesus on this one and get this stuff out of our backpacks!

Gospel Grit Challenge: If you do not conquer lust, lust will conquer you. Do you need help in the area of lust? Do you know who to turn to? Do you know where to get help?

T—MATTHEW 5:29: "IF YOUR RIGHT EYE MAKES YOU STUMBLE, TEAR IT OUT."

(See also Matthew 5:30; two references.)

I put these two verses together because though one emphasizes eliminating the eye and the other eliminating a hand, I believe Jesus is making the same point. Jesus is pointing to a radical change of heart and life. He is saying to those who really want to follow Him, "There are some things in your life that I will not tolerate."

Certainly, we live in a culture that places a high value on tolerance. Jesus places a high value on love, which is the difference between His teaching and that of the teachers of our culture. Cutting off hands and gouging out eyes is not tolerance at all.

I remember the first time I heard the story of a man named Origen, who lived around the year 200. A professor told me of Origen's devotion to God, which he expressed by sleeping on the hard floor, eating only bread and water, and castrating himself in order to be sexually pure! Yikes! Did God tell Origen to do such a thing? I doubt it. But if He did, that is one obedient man!

Do you really think Jesus is asking us to cut out eyes and hands if we cannot control what they see and what they touch? I don't. Jesus is teaching us the importance of eternity. Jesus is teaching us the importance of not living for the moment. Jesus is teaching us that the issues He addresses in life are serious. Jesus wants us to give Him our best so that we can experience His best in us. Jesus is not talking about a bad eye or a mischievous hand, He is talking about a clean heart. When He transforms our hearts, he spares our limbs and organs!

Gospel Grit Challenge: Do you struggle with bad behavior? Is it an issue of both the mind and the heart? Discuss ways you can move toward a cleaner mind and a cleaner heart.

T—MATTHEW 5:32: "EVERYONE WHO DIVORCES HIS WIFE, EXCEPT FOR THE CAUSE OF UNCHASTITY, MAKES HER COMMIT ADULTERY; AND WHOEVER MARRIES A DIVORCED WOMAN COMMITS ADULTERY."

(See also Matthew 19:9, Mark 10:9, Mark 10:11–12, and Luke 16:18; five references.)

If divorce has hit your home, this is most likely a difficult subject for you. If divorce has not hit your home, it is not as difficult. That's just the way it is. The statistics on divorce are staggering. Within church ranks, they are not good either. I am not advocating solutions to divorce. I am not advocating anything other than what Jesus tells us. I believe Jesus is telling us that anything other than adultery as grounds for divorce is out of bounds.

I used to play quite a bit of golf. Now I am only a legend in my own mind. There are several events in a round that can ruin a really good score. Three-putting a green can ruin a good score. Shanks can ruin a good score. Hitting the ball in the sand can ruin a good score. But nothing can ruin a score faster than hitting the ball out of bounds. That event carries with it a two-stroke penalty and can change your score faster than most anything else.

Here in the Gospels, Jesus is telling us that God has made one provision that legitimizes divorce. (Physical abuse and breaking the law are also out of bounds; other Scriptures apply.) I don't really like it either, because there are some other circumstances where it would seem to me that being divorced is the only option. Again, I am not taking sides; I am simply highlighting what Jesus told us.

> *Gospel Grit Challenge: If you have divorce in your family, begin by forgiving yourself. Then forgive anyone else who needs forgiving. Then think of someone you know who has been divorced who would benefit from an encouraging word, and go encourage that person before reading another page. That is discipleship in action!*

T—MATTHEW 5:34–36: "MAKE NO OATH AT ALL."

(See also Matthew 5:37; two references.)

We are to live our lives in such a way that what comes out of our mouth is truth, so much so that oaths are not required when truth is applied. This makes perfect sense to me. I am sure it made perfect sense to Jesus too, as He is the one who said it!

We live in a culture plagued with lies and half-truths, which are also lies. We live in a culture that has butchered integrity by changing its meaning. Jesus said our responses to people are to be as clear as yes and no. We are to be His followers, marked by integrity and honesty and purity.

We all can think of examples of lying. We can think of a time when we have lied. We understand the nature of lying. We are to be people of truth, telling the truth and speaking the truth. We need to think of examples of when the truth was told and the good that it did. Instead of so quickly thinking about the bad, let's spend more time thinking about noble speech.

I was told by a lawyer friend there are three answers that a witness can give: "Yes," "No," and "I do not know." He told me he prefers the latter because it is usually the most accurate answer. I believe Jesus wants us to be dead honest and accurate when we speak. This is what is at the heart of this teaching.

Gospel Grit Challenge: "May the words of my mouth and the meditation of my heart be acceptable in Thy sight, O Lord, my rock and my Redeemer" (Psalm 19:14).

T—MATTHEW 5:39: "DO NOT RESIST AN EVIL PERSON; BUT WHOEVER SLAPS YOU ON YOUR RIGHT CHEEK, TURN THE OTHER TO HIM ALSO."

(See also Luke 6:27–31; two references.)

I told a story earlier in this book of when a bully hit me in the face and knocked me to the ground. I have to be honest with you: to ask me to stand up and tell him to hit me again to balance out the bruise on the other side of my face would have been asking a bit much, that day or any day. Yet, Jesus teaches us to offer both cheeks to our enemies.

What Jesus is asking of us takes strength, not weakness. What Jesus is asking of us takes courage. He is asking us to take the high road. Why is it that Jesus is always asking us to do what is hard? He rarely seems to lead us down the road of easy. At least, that is the way it is in my life.

This strength Jesus is teaching is not an outer strength; rather, it's an inner strength. Outer strength comes from the flesh. Inner strength comes from the Spirit. Jesus is teaching us to rely on the Holy Spirit. In the situation He paints, Jesus is using a scenario that usually plays out in the flesh. Jesus turns that model upside down and tells us to live within the realm of the Spirit. This then becomes the point: to be controlled and under the influence of the Holy Spirit in our lives. This is the only way we can deliver on this teaching. There is no other way; we just are not that good. Ultimately, Jesus is telling us to rely on Him, especially in those times when the way of the flesh is more desirable.

Gospel Grit Challenge: Give some thought to developing inner strength further in your life. Think about ways you can move from living in the flesh to living in the Spirit.

T—MATTHEW 5:40: "IF ANYONE WANTS TO SUE YOU, AND TAKE YOUR SHIRT, LET HIM HAVE YOUR COAT ALSO."

This is a tough one because it isn't fair. I had a professor in my doctoral work teach me a very important truth: he said, "Life isn't fair, get over it." This teaching from Jesus is not about fairness. I think even Jesus would acknowledge that fact. It is a teaching about what Jesus wants us to do, often for reasons we will not ever know. There are some things He tells us that don't make much sense. The point is not for us to fully understand as much as it is to fully obey.

Our church was named in a lawsuit several years ago because a boy got hurt at a youth camp our church participated in. None of our kids were involved in the injury. None of our leaders were involved. But because we were there, we were named in essence as an accomplice to the crime. We were sued for $2,000,000 for something we didn't do. And the plaintiff won. The following day, our insurance company dropped us. Life is not fair.

Gospel Grit Challenge: Identify something in your life that was not fair. Now, you have a choice to either become bitter or better. Figure out how you can become better and release the bitterness to God.

T—MATTHEW 5:41: "WHOEVER FORCES YOU TO GO ONE MILE, GO WITH HIM TWO."

In Jesus's day, Roman soldiers would sometimes force Jewish bystanders to carry their baggage. In our own day, we sometimes end up having to help people when we don't want to, or being forced into situations that are inconvenient for us. Maybe somebody at work requires help, and we don't think we should have to give it. Or we have to do the dishes when we're tired and we think it should be somebody else's job. Or maintaining a particular relationship feels like more trouble than it's worth.

Jesus is asking us to go twice as far as we are being forced to go by someone. What do you suppose Jesus is after? Perhaps He wants us to be salt and light in darkness, as He stated previously. Perhaps He wants us to love and not fight. Perhaps He knows something we don't. Perhaps He knows human nature and knows that it's in our best interests to do exactly as He says.

Again and again, I will remind you I did not write these things, I just recorded them so we can see clearly what a follower of Jesus is supposed to look like. Some pieces to the Jesus puzzle are hard to put into their proper place. Yet if one piece is missing, the entire puzzle is incomplete.

Gospel Grit Challenge: Are you walking with someone in life whom you are not enjoying one single bit? Is it possible God will ask you to walk further with that person? Is it possible it is not about you but about the other person? Consider the benefits of doing it Jesus's way.

T—MATTHEW 5:42: "GIVE TO HIM WHO ASKS OF YOU, AND DO NOT TURN AWAY FROM HIM WHO WANTS TO BORROW FROM YOU."

Matthew 5–7 gives some really tough lessons to practice. Just when you get one of them mastered, you go to the next page and discover another tough assignment. Yet they are all part of being a follower of Jesus Christ.

Something should be said about expectations regarding this teaching. Lower your expectations and lower the degree of hurt. There must be a balance between giving to someone and enabling someone. When you read the whole of Scripture, you can see that Jesus does not advocate enabling people so they can continue harmful behavior; rather, He teaches generosity.

Generosity is at the heart of the Gospels. Everything Jesus did came from a heart of generosity. His most generous act was the cross, where He died for the whole world.

I believe it is fair to say when lending or loaning money, or anything for that matter, that it's right to teach the borrowers responsibility and hold them to a high standard of accountability. In this we are truly helping to develop their character and to build their integrity.

Gospel Grit Challenge: In what ways can you be more generous? How can Christians better cultivate a culture and climate of generosity?

T—MATTHEW 5:48: "THEREFORE, YOU ARE TO BE PERFECT, AS YOUR HEAVENLY FATHER IS PERFECT."

My favorite play in football at any level is when the quarterback throws the bomb. One Sunday, I used this as an illustration during one of my messages. I will never forget the dear retired missionary lady who was so upset with me after the service that she came up and told me as much. She thought I was talking about bombing something, as in a war! After I explained it to her, we both had a good laugh.

In football (just in case there is someone reading this who would respond like that missionary lady), throwing the bomb is when the quarterback drops back in the pocket and waits, and while he is waiting for what seems an eternity, his receivers are running down the field as fast as they can and as far as they can. It is at that moment the quarterback throws the ball as far as he can, hoping someone on his team will catch it. That is throwing the bomb. I wish it happened on every play.

In reviewing all these things, Jesus is showing us and telling us that some things are like a draw play, some are like a screen pass, some are like a fullback plowing up the middle, some are an end around (I like this play too), and once in a great while, Jesus throws the bomb. That is what this verse is in my opinion: it is going for broke.

"Perfect" is about as daunting a word as you can get, especially when it comes to behavior and especially when the comparison is to God Almighty! Yet Jesus tells us to be perfect. He would not ask us to do something we cannot do, right? None of us can do this one on our own, which is the point. Once again, Jesus is seeking to draw us into synch with Him and asking that we allow Him to lead from the center out. He leads from within my heart, and as I follow Him, I am able to accomplish His teaching. Do not be overwhelmed; just think about getting in synch with Jesus. We are told to follow Him. The mistake people make is following Him at a distance. He meant for us to follow Him up close and personal!

> *Gospel Grit Challenge: What keeps you from running down the field of life expecting to catch what Jesus throws to you? Give Him your fears and hesitations out of your backpack today. Start running down the field. There is a ball in the air with your name on it!*

T—MATTHEW 6:3: "WHEN YOU GIVE TO THE POOR, DO NOT LET YOUR LEFT HAND KNOW WHAT YOUR RIGHT HAND IS DOING."

(See also Matthew 19:21, Mark 10:2, Luke 4:18–19, Luke 18:22, Luke 21:2, and John 12:8; seven references.)

There are other references to the poor in the Gospels besides those listed above. I have highlighted some to show that Jesus often addresses this particular people group. In the United States of America, for the most part we live in a land of plenty. We really do. I often hear people say they are poor, when what they really mean is that they do not have as much as their friends. If you have food to eat and a place to sleep, you are rich. That would probably include prisoners too! (Have you ever seen jail conditions in other countries or studied the history of prisons? Even our prisons are rich!)

While Jesus lifts out a people group in this verse, His emphasis is not so much on the poor as it is on the one who gives to the poor. We are instructed to give in such a way as not to bring attention to ourselves. We have many examples of people who have given much, and we have heard their inspiring stories. At the same time, I believe there are far more stories out there waiting to be told when we get to heaven, stories of people who have given and whose gifts have been kept secret except for an audience of one—God Himself!

Jesus also makes an assumption here that we *will* give to the poor. It is to be a part of our DNA. Giving to the poor is the right thing to do. Broadcasting our giving is the wrong thing to do. It's like praying in public so everyone can see our piety. Nobody is really impressed, especially God.

Jesus teaches silent generosity. Let's be good students of His teaching.

Gospel Grit Challenge: Thank God for all He has blessed you with. Scour through your backpack and find all the blessings God has given you over your lifetime. You will discover you are blessed! Think of people you can give to in this country. Identify another country you can give to and reasons for selecting that country.

T—MATTHEW 6:6: "WHEN YOU PRAY, GO INTO YOUR INNER ROOM, CLOSE YOUR DOOR AND PRAY TO YOUR FATHER WHO IS IN SECRET."

(See also Matthew 6:7, Matthew 6:9–13, Matthew 14:23, Matthew 17:21, Matthew 19:15, Matthew 21:3, Matthew 21:22, Matthew 26:36, Matthew 26:39, Matthew 26:41, Matthew 26:42, Matthew 26:44, Mark 1:35, Mark 6:46, Mark 9:29, Mark 11:17, Mark 11:24, Mark 11:25, Mark 14:32, Mark 14:35, Mark 14:38, Mark 14:39, Luke 6:12, Luke 9:18, Luke 9:28, Luke 11:1, Luke 11:2–4, Luke 15:16, Luke 19:46, Luke 22:40, Luke 22:41, Luke 22:44, Luke 22:46, and John 17:2–26; thirty-five references.)

As you process this look at the life of Jesus in the Gospels, you will begin to see some big themes. This teaching in Matthew 6:6, along with over thirty other references to prayer, is certainly one of the largest.

There are some huge misunderstandings concerning prayer. One, God is a genie with a lamp we rub to get what we wish. In actuality, prayer is about lining up with the will of God. Two, prayer is just us talking. The truth is that prayer is not one way, but two ways. We seem to spend more time talking than listening. I suppose it is because we do not recognize the Lord's voice. Jesus addresses this too in the Gospels. Three, prayer is all about getting stuff. The reality is that prayer is not so much about getting stuff as it is about relationship.

Prayer is a relationship with God. Yes, prayer confesses our need for God. But prayer also acknowledges God's desire to be with us. He is forever reclaiming what was lost in the garden of Eden.

Many people who love God practice this teaching far better than others. In fact, you will not know it if they do practice this teaching well, because they are doing it in secret in their closet. It is important that we pray and that we pray before the Lord in the most intimate of places. This is the nature of relationships.

Likely, the people receiving the largest rewards in heaven will be the behind-the-scenes people. Churches that flourish often give credit to their leaders. But I suspect much of the credit should go to the prayer warriors who quietly and faithfully go about the business of intimacy with God. They understand and experience the essence of a covenant relationship with God.

Gospel Grit Challenge: Where is your prayer closet? Does prayer make a difference? Which accomplishes more good…praying for those considering abortions or picketing an abortion clinic? Asking this question of others should make for some hearty discussion! If your knees get sore from kneeling, use your backpack. That may be the best use for having it with you!

T—MATTHEW 6:14: "IF YOU FORGIVE OTHERS…YOUR HEAVENLY FATHER WILL ALSO FORGIVE YOU."

(See also Matthew 6:15, Matthew 9:2, Matthew 18:22, Matthew 18:35, Mark 2:5, Mark 11:26, Luke 5:32, Luke 6:37, Luke 7:47, Luke 12:8–10, Luke 15:10, Luke 17:3–4, Luke 23:34, John 8:7, John 8:11, and John 20:23; seventeen references.)

Forgiveness is another key theme in the teachings of Jesus. He puts great emphasis on His forgiveness of us and our forgiveness of one another. It is much easier for us to receive His forgiveness than it is to extend forgiveness to another.

Grudges, bitterness, anger, harsh words, lack of peace, murmurings, factions, division, and hatred are all things that can be present when we fail to forgive. Forgiveness is essential when dealing with the human race. We are fallen. Without forgiveness we are doomed.

Matthew 6:14 is especially piercing because Jesus connects His forgiveness with our forgiveness of others. What a dirty trick! Sometimes it feels really good *not* to forgive. Jesus knew this would be part of our nature, so He showed us that as we are extended grace from God, we should extend grace toward others.

We can all easily come up with a list of people we have forgiven and people we do not want to forgive for what they have done to us. Interestingly, when we forgive, we can testify to good things that have followed forgiveness. Sadly, we know exactly the grip Satan has on us when we choose not to forgive. Choose forgiveness.

Gospel Grit Challenge: Recount all the sin God has forgiven in your life. Give Him thanks for His kindness to you. Now, is there any way you can extend that same grace and kindness to someone who is under your skin?

T—MATTHEW 6:19: "DO NOT STORE UP FOR YOURSELVES TREASURES ON EARTH."

(See also Matthew 6:20, Matthew 6:24, Matthew 7:6, Matthew 10:9, Matthew 17:24–25, Matthew 21:12, Matthew 22:21, Mark 6:7–9, Mark 10:21, Mark

10:23, Mark 11:15–16, Mark 12:17, Mark 12:41, Luke 6:38, Luke 12:15, Luke 12:21, Luke 12:22, Luke 12:24, Luke 12:27, Luke 12:29, Luke 12:23, Luke 14:33, Luke 16:13, Luke 18:24, Luke 20:15, and John 2:15; twenty-seven references.)

It has been noted that references to money in the Bible top out at two thousand passages, while Scriptures on prayer, heaven, and hell number far less. Jesus knew the DNA of humanity. He knew that issues relating to money would be one of our two big struggles. Do you know what the other big one is? That would be issues relating to sex. What a huge surprise that is.

Even today, issues like tithing, budgeting, debt, retirement, and credit cards are bringing heaviness on many people. It does not need to be that way. Jesus came to set us free from ourselves and from the love of money. Money is not the answer to a great life. Money is a tool toward a great life. How we manage it is what matters. Jesus continuously talks about stewardship, which is how we manage our money.

The subtitle of my book describes Jesus as a man who was unemployed and homeless. Why should we listen to someone with those credentials? Because the man who was homeless and carrying a backpack is the King of Kings and the Lord of Lords. Jesus is *fully* God. He is qualified to talk about money!

Who do you think invented business? God. Who do you think created commerce? God. Who do you think created agriculture? God. Who do you think prepared that land flowing with milk and honey and vineyards that the Israelites did not plant? God. God is the source from which the milk and honey flowed. In American history, who do you think created the wealth for ranchers with all those animals? God is the Creator of ranches, and God is the first cowboy!

What about the twenty-first century? Believe me, the God of the universe understands the Internet, social networking, and banking. Always remember what the streets of heaven are made of! We somehow think God is old-fashioned, irrelevant, out of touch, and out of date. He is God! He knows about money. He is its Creator.

I urge you to look up each of the verses referenced at the top of this teaching. Not all the verses say the same thing. However, they are all related topically, and together they give us a crystal-clear picture of what it means to follow Jesus in the area of finances.

> *Gospel Grit Challenge: What do the Scriptures say specifically about your personal money issues? If you want to be blessed by God, you must tithe as a starting point. What other financial areas do you need to grow or be obedient in?*

T—MATTHEW 6:25: "DO NOT WORRY ABOUT YOUR LIFE AS TO WHAT YOU SHOULD EAT OR WHAT YOU SHALL DRINK, NOR FOR YOUR BODY, AS TO WHAT YOU SHALL PUT ON."

(See also Matthew 6:34, Matthew 10:19, and Luke 21:34; four references.)

You may be a person who worries, or there is probably someone in your family who worries. I am not referencing an occasional bout of anxiety; I am talking about worry to the level that it becomes a life-shaping issue.

Jesus is in a unique position to talk about worry. He has no address, a backpack at best, no paycheck coming in, yet He doesn't seem to be worried. So He is passing on advice about life we can benefit from: do not worry!

It is likely that most things we worry about never materialize, yet we worry. We know God will take care of us, yet we worry. We know we have had everything we needed in the past, yet we worry. Worry robs us of joy.

Jesus is specifically referencing worry about food, drink, and clothing. But the principle is true across the board. Think about all the things we worry about that are outside these three. We worry about just about everything, especially our children (for good reason, I might add!).

So the question must be asked: how do we move away from worry if worrying is a natural way of life? I would love to do the pastor thing and give you some answers. However, I am not the guy handing out the advice. I am not the guy with a backpack on my back wandering throughout Israel with no job and no place to pick up my mail. Jesus seems to tell us something we need to be doing with no real explanation on how to pull it off. Maybe His response would be put a pack on your back, go for a three-year hike, and leave no forwarding address!

Seriously, how *do* we pull this one off? Picture the scene with me. Jesus is in the midst of teaching, and this is one of many subjects being taught. His answers are not in a list but in constant motion as He moves in and out of the crowds. He is teaching us not to find the answers of life in a list of dos and don'ts, but rather to walk with Him and let things work out.

I worry tons! As I studied this teaching, I have been trying to do better at taking Jesus literally and just walking with Him in life. To my amazement, doing it His way works! Give it a try, or you may worry yourself right into a nursing home.

Gospel Grit Challenge: Make a list of things you worry about, load them up in your backpack, and start walking with Jesus. You will be so happy just to be with Him, what you carry in your backpack will not be such a burden.

T—MATTHEW 6:33: "SEEK FIRST HIS KINGDOM AND HIS RIGHTEOUS-
NESS."

(See also Luke 12:31, Luke 16:10, John 3:3, and John 3:5; five references.)

This teaching, along with four other passages, mentions the importance to Jesus of His kingdom and His righteousness. These are two important themes in His life and teaching.

His kingdom is important to Jesus because it is His domain. Our domains are always important. Perhaps Jesus is not so concerned about this life because His domain is large and forever. Perhaps He could wander through the land as He did because He knew it was going to be short-lived.

His righteousness is important to Jesus because it goes to the issue of relationship. Walking with Jesus for three intense years is critically important, because during this time we are able to capture what it means to be a follower of Jesus in real time in a real relationship. Jesus would have us understand the importance of His righteousness because it goes to the core of who He is and what He wants us to become. It is not as simple as reading a book. We must walk with Him.

I teach at Northwest University in an adjunct position. I enjoy the opportunity to teach college students. Several of my courses include some of the material from this book. Many students in the class will receive high marks from me and will ultimately receive an A for the course. But mastering the class does not mean they have mastered walking with Jesus. One masters walking with Jesus by walking with Jesus.

Likewise, I am teaching some of this book at my church over the next year, walking through the passages and some of the Gospel Grit Challenges. I have asked everyone to think about what is in their backpack. This does not guarantee success. Success in discipleship is not defined by grades or how much we memorize or anything other than walking with Jesus. In this book I am merely walking you through the Gospels, opening a door for you to walk with Jesus. It's up to you to get through that door and onto the road.

Gospel Grit Challenge: What can you do to bring righteousness and kingdom living more fully into your life?

T—MATTHEW 7:1: "DO NOT JUDGE."

We judge one another all day long. We judge people in the elevator by sizing them up. We judge fellow employees. We judge people in the grocery store and places where we play. We judge people at church (*especially* at church). We judge our children and spouse when they mess up. We judge our pastor on a regular basis. We judge God when we do not agree with what He is doing. We judge all the time.

Is Jesus telling us to do something that is not attainable? That would not be in His nature or character. But how can we not judge when judging is a part of how a human being thinks?

We can begin implementing this teaching by walking in other people's shoes. Until we have done that, we have no room or right to judge. (Another way of putting this is to wear their backpack.) This will help us to understand what others are experiencing. Second, we can pray for people when we would otherwise judge them.

Maybe you find that the above habits don't make enough difference. What if our incentive to break this nasty habit of judging was to acknowledge our desire to be Jesus-pleasers? We want to please Jesus. Let's start thinking about how our behavior affects Jesus. Is He pleased when we judge others? Based on this passage, apparently not!

I hope you agree with me that we rarely know the whole story, and when we do know the whole story, we still do not know the fallout. What kind of a world would it be if we could truly accept and love people without judging them? Can you imagine how much better church life would be? Can you imagine how much better our world would be? More immediately, can you imagine how much happier *you* would be if you stopped judging people?

Gospel Grit Challenge: Who do you judge? Why do you judge them? Are you ready to stop the madness? Get all judgments out of your backpack and give them to Jesus right away!

T—MATTHEW 7:5: "FIRST TAKE THE LOG OUT OF YOUR OWN EYE."

(See also Luke 13:24; two references.)

This teaching is a separate issue from the previous teaching on judgment, though they are certainly connected. Allow me to explain.

When we make judgments about people, we are judging the behavior we see them doing through the lenses we wear. This teaching of Jesus is not about what people do, but about the lenses we wear. We make most situations look either good or bad based on what we choose to see.

Congress is an excellent example. Have you ever seen a government so divided? We watch with amazement the comments made based on the lenses being worn by each side at the time. Of course, I think one lens is the right lens and the other lens is the wrong lens! But this is the whole problem.

Taking the log out of our own eye means we are to take the log out of our own eye. And you thought I was going to try to explain what Jesus meant! This book is not about what He meant as much as it is about what He showed us and told us.

When we think someone else is in error, our starting point should be to look in the mirror. When we want to point a finger at someone, there are three more fingers pointing right back at us!

The imagery Jesus is placing before us is huge. He is not talking about a sliver requiring tweezers. Jesus is talking about logs requiring a chainsaw. After you cut up the log, feel free to throw it in Jesus's backpack. He is carrying other people's planks too!

Gospel Grit Challenge: How can we move from pride to humility? What are some steps that can be taken? This is really what Jesus is talking about.

T—MATTHEW 7:7: "ASK, AND IT WILL BE GIVEN TO YOU; SEEK, AND YOU WILL FIND; KNOCK, AND IT WILL BE OPENED TO YOU."

(See also Luke 11:9, John 14:13–15, John 15:7, and John 16:24; five references.)

I recognize this falls under the category of prayer, which we've already talked about elsewhere, but because it is a classic teaching of Jesus, I have chosen to let it stand on its own. There are at least five other passages of Scripture I have identified in the Gospels that focus on the word *ask*.

Wouldn't it be sad to get to heaven and realize there were things that could have been entirely different for us on earth if we had just asked?

I am a father, and I have a father. I remember as a child always asking my dad for things I could not provide for myself. My favorite time to beg was at Christmas. We did not have a lot of money (I later learned) growing up, and what we got for Christmas was a really big deal. For a nine-year-old boy, there is not a better gift than a BB gun. I begged my dad for a gun before I went to bed, and then when I was in bed I begged God to talk to my dad. I figured between the two I had a pretty good chance of getting a BB gun for Christmas. (Looking back, I am not too sure what God had to do with what was under the tree!)

Christmas morning came, and under our tree I saw a box about three feet long and about eight inches wide. It had to be my BB gun. Had I not asked for that gift, I probably would have gotten something like a coat. I am so glad I asked my dad for that BB gun.

Jesus isn't Santa, and Christmas is only one day a year, yet Jesus tells us we do not have much under the tree because we do not ask enough. This may sound a bit strange, but start asking. I believe He is addressing us on a primarily spiritual level, though the physical is a part of it too. The point is, spend more time with Jesus, and in your conversations with Him make your asking more natural and not so manufactured like a Christmas list. He wants to hear from you.

Gospel Grit Challenge: What kind of faith do you need to grow to seek God in the really big areas of your life? Lord, help our unbelief!

T—MATTHEW 7:12: "TREAT PEOPLE THE SAME WAY YOU WANT THEM TO TREAT YOU."

I am writing at this time at my mother-in-law's house. We live about 150 miles from one another. Last year my father-in-law went home to be with the Lord. This is her first full year without her husband of well over sixty years. Two friends who are staying at nearby resorts have asked what it is I am doing at her house, meaning, "Can you come spend time with us?" As it turns out, I am not doing very much at her house—just spending time with her. The same thing my friends are asking of me, my wife and I are doing with my mother-in-law.

On this three-year hike Jesus is taking us on, He asks us to do various things along the way. But more than anything else, He appears to want us to spend time with Him. I am reminded of God in the garden of Eden, where He spent time with Adam and Eve. The day came when God wanted to spend time with His creation, but His creation had disobeyed. God asked, "Where are you?" I think that is one of the most profound questions in the entire Bible.

Jesus is asking us to walk with Him. If you want to know what you will accomplish, maybe the answer is that you will just be with Him. Jesus wants us to walk with Him more than He wants us to accomplish a list of tasks. Are we up to the challenge?

Gospel Grit Challenge: How much time do you spend per day with Jesus? Will you spend more time with Him in the future? Pull out your calendar and start penciling in time with Jesus. After all, it's hard to follow someone you are not with!

T—MATTHEW 7:13: "ENTER THROUGH THE NARROW GATE."

(See also Luke 13:24; two references.)

The potential implications of this teaching are staggering. When we take this passage and put it with the verse that follows it, we should become utterly sober. The verse that follows is not for followers of Jesus Christ. It is for those who choose not to follow Him. It says, "For the gate is small, and the way is narrow that leads to life, and few are those who find it."

Why would a God who loves us so much make it so hard to get through the gate? Or is the gate only narrow to those who do not follow Jesus Christ? The gate is narrow, but wide enough to go through if we are following Jesus.

I am claustrophobic. When I was a child, I could not stand being held down for any reason. I would go berserk. I have not tested my phobia in recent years, but I have a feeling not much has changed.

On October 5, 1991, I fell off a ladder some twenty-four feet to the ground, breaking my back in two places. It is a miracle I am walking today. After I arrived at the hospital by ambulance, the doctor ordered a test that found me strapped to a gurney slowly being ushered into a skinny, narrow, hellish tube. Had I not been in so much pain, I would have freaked out. The entire experience was memorable and awful all at the same time.

When we who follow Jesus Christ go to heaven, I do not picture our entrance through the gate being anything like that test for broken bones. I believe it is going to be a grand and glorious entrance. By that time, Jesus will have shaped and molded us into His image so that what used to be a narrow gate now seems wide as the ocean, not because the bar has been lowered but because our obedience to Him has been rewarded.

Much has been written about the road less traveled. I believe the road less traveled leads to the gate less traveled. It is that narrow gate at the end of our road on the road few choose to travel. If we follow Him, this gate will be plenty wide enough. The key is to follow Him.

Gospel Grit Challenge: Is your life being lived in strict obedience to the Gospels, or are you fudging? When we fudge on a diet, the weight does not come off, and we are not likely to fit into our jeans. Likewise, if we are not really following Jesus, then we really are not likely to fit through the narrow gate. What changes in your heart need to be made to get into shape to fit through that narrow gate? Is your backpack getting in the way? Do you know to throw a few things out of it and replace them with repentance and faith?

T—MATTHEW 7:15: "BEWARE OF THE FALSE PROPHETS."

(See also Matthew 24:23, Matthew 24:26, and Mark 13:21; four references.)
I am giving a message this Sunday on this subject of false prophets.

I have never specifically covered this subject before from the pulpit, but it's an important one. Whenever Jesus says for us to beware, what He really means is for us to beware!

Children are warned repeatedly not to touch a hot stove. Teenagers are told repeatedly not to drive carelessly. We are told by everyone not to drink and drive. (I have a simple solution to this one, which is not to drink at all!) Now we have commercials on television reminding us not to text and drive, showing us pictures of families who have been killed in car accidents while they were texting. These are all examples of the word *beware*.

Jesus gives us plenty of examples in the Gospels, and God gives us plenty more examples in the rest of the Bible, of what happens when we ignore the warnings placed before us. It will always end in disaster. It will always end in people getting hurt.

We are told as children never to talk to strangers. This is good advice. But it seems to me the problem with false prophets is not the stranger who tries to woo us away from Jesus; it's people we know who tell us what we want to hear that takes us away from Jesus.

Jesus is asking us not only to be careful, but to beware. It is a strong word, a strong warning, a strong teaching that has been given to us for our benefit.

Do you remember the account of Reverend Jim Jones, who had nearly one thousand people follow him to a commune in Africa only to drink the Kool-Aid and die of poisoning? Jesus is telling us to beware because there may be someone within our reach who is preparing us to drink the Kool-Aid! Perhaps a cause minus Scripture or a charismatic person who espouses a teaching minus the Scripture. Or worse, someone who uses the Scripture without teaching everything Jesus has told us and showed us and thus uses the Bible to teach lies.

Gospel Grit Challenge: Are you a student of the Bible? Are you willing to change your life around in such a way as to spend much more time in Bible study? What is more important to you than studying the Bible? What prevents you from studying the Bible in a way that requires far more than the minimum amount of energy with Jesus and in the Word? Anything preventing us from following Jesus needs to be taken out of our backpack!

T—MATTHEW 7:21: "NOT EVERYONE WHO SAYS TO ME, 'LORD, LORD,' WILL ENTER THE KINGDOM OF HEAVEN, BUT HE WHO DOES THE WILL OF MY FATHER WHO IS IN HEAVEN WILL ENTER."

(See also Matthew 12:50, Mark 3:35, Mark 14:36, and Luke 22:42; five references.)

My focus for this teaching is on the word "will." However, I have to say just a few words about what else is said in this verse. The consequences of *not* doing the will of God should be alarming to all of us. Following Jesus means to follow the will of God. We know it is the will of God to be a living sacrifice according to Romans 12:1–2. We know it is God's will to abstain from sexual immorality according to 1 Thessalonians 4:1–8. And we know it is the will of God to love His Son, Jesus, with every ounce of our being. If we can get this one right, we are likely to get a lot of other things right also.

We each have a will. I am not particularly interested in doctrine at this point, differentiating between my will and my choice and God's will and sovereignty and divine providence. I want to keep it more basic than that because I believe Jesus was not making a statement about doctrine so much as He was making a statement about our DNA. More to the point, Jesus is attacking our stubbornness.

Some people are more stubborn than others. Those who are the most stubborn have the strongest wills. We who are in that category need to sit up and pay close attention to this teaching. How easily and quickly do we follow what we want because we are so sure we are always or most always right? It happens all of the time. A strong will is both a blessing and a curse. When our will is angled away from following Jesus, it always ends up hurting us. Those of us who have a strong will need to really follow Jesus closely so that we can constantly check our will at the door.

Our will, that is the part of our will that would turn us away from following Jesus with something else that catches our eye, is another great thing to toss out of the backpack as we travel along the road with Jesus, replacing it with a will to follow Him.

One of the passages of Scripture I cite above presents Jesus as the example of giving away His will to the Father. Nobody who is healthy wants to die. Jesus was young and healthy when it was time for Him to face death. (He was also homeless and unemployed. By the way, when they hung Him on the cross, His backpack went with Him. It turns out the only thing He had room for in His backpack was our sin. All the other stuff fell out along the road somewhere in Israel.)

Gospel Grit Challenge: What is in your life that you need to give to Jesus so you can really start to follow Him? If you are not ready now to give it to Him, what do you think it will take for you to make a surrender of your will to His?

T—MATTHEW 7:24: "EVERYONE WHO HEARS THESE WORDS OF MINE AND ACTS ON THEM, MAY BE COMPARED TO A WISE MAN."

(See also Matthew 7:26, Matthew 13:3, Matthew 13:18–23, Matthew 13:24–30, Matthew 13:31–32, Matthew 13:33, Matthew 13:36–50, Matthew 24:32, Mark 3:23, Mark 4:10, Mark 4:33, Mark 4:34, Mark 12:1, Mark 13:28, Luke 5:36, Luke 6:39, Luke 6:47–49, Luke 8:4, Luke 10:37, Luke 12:16, Luke 13:6, Luke 14:7, Luke 15:3, Luke 18:1, Luke 18:9, Luke 19:11, Luke 20:9, and Luke 21:29; twenty-nine references.)

Every child loves to hear a story. Every adult loves to hear a good story. Stories make sense because they mirror reality. Jesus often taught using parables. I have identified twenty-nine passages where Jesus used a parable to teach a significant spiritual truth that would help people follow Him more closely. Parables are stories with a spiritual meaning.

Parables paint a picture. My aunt is an artist, and I have a picture hanging in my office at home that she painted in 1959, the year I was born. I love the picture because it takes me to the scene she painted. Words are not required for me to understand her message. Jesus really wanted to make sure we understood His words, so He used parables.

The relationship Jesus desires to have with us is more than words on a piece of paper. Relationships are built on the canvas of life. Jesus is the artist. He brings us to life with Him as He shapes the story and paints pictures that go beyond scholarly words or explanations.

I remember a story I read in seminary about an artist who painted a small bird in a large tree in the bottom right-hand corner of a canvas. When he submitted his picture to be judged along with his peers, they began murmuring about his work. He was ridiculed for not finishing his painting. When asked by the judge why he hadn't finished his work, he told the judge to look closely at the title of the painting: *Room to Fly.*

This is what Jesus does with parables. Following Jesus does not restrict us, it sets us free! He's given us wings to fly on the canvas of life. Parables give us understanding. With understanding comes room to fly.

A story is told of an elderly woman desiring to give her little goldfish a birthday gift. She filled up her bathtub with water and dumped her fish into the tub. To her amazement, the fish continued to swim in the same small circles it swam in when in the small bowl. Jesus offers freedom from a life of restriction and entanglement brought on by the lies of Satan. Jesus desires for us to swim the ocean. Satan offers us a stinky swamp.

God has given us skies in which to soar. Parables are the keys that unbind our wings. We are not chickens with our heads to the ground, pecking at underweight bugs. We are eagles, and eagles are meant to soar the skies under heaven. Parables become the wings that allow us to fly with Jesus.

Gospel Grit Challenge: Where do you fit on the canvas of life? Jesus has given you wings to fly. What do you plan on doing for Him? Think big!

T—MATTHEW 7:29: "HE TAUGHT THEM AS ONE HAVING AUTHORITY."

(*See also Matthew 10:7, Matthew 11:1, Matthew 13:54, Matthew 13:57, Matthew 21:23, Matthew 22:33, Mark 1:14, Mark 1:21, Mark 1:38, Mark 1:39, Mark 2:2, Mark 2:13, Mark 4:1, Mark 4:2, Mark 4:9, Mark 6:2, Mark 6:6, Mark 6:34, Mark 8:31, Mark 9:31, Mark 10:1, Mark 12:14, Mark 12:35, Mark 12:37, Luke 4:15, Luke 4:16, Luke 4:18–19, Luke 4:20, Luke 4:24, Luke 4:31, Luke 4:43, Luke 4:44, Luke 5:3, Luke 5:17, Luke 6:6, Luke 7:1, Luke 8:1, Luke 10:1, Luke 10:2, Luke 13:10, Luke 13:22, Luke 19:47, Luke 20:1, Luke 21:37, John 6:59, John 7:14, John 8:2, John 8:6, John 8:8, John 8:20, and John 8:30; fifty-two references.*)

Wow! The Gospels record Jesus preaching or teaching fifty-two times. Thus far in this study, we have seen that He spent the majority of His time healing, preaching, and teaching. Jesus was teaching and preaching every moment He had. That is what the Gospels are all about. They are about Jesus telling us everything we need to know for living life. Further, He showed us how to live life as well.

As a child I would play the game "Simon Says." It was a fun game for me because I liked tricking people when it was my turn to be Simon. I have some news for all of us: Jesus never tries to trick us. His desire is for us to mirror what He does. His desire for us is to be completely synchronized with Him. It is at this point that we become salt and light to a very lost world.

The point of so many recorded passages telling us that Jesus was teaching and preaching is for us to capture our need to listen and learn. Listening and learning is one of the most important aspects of following Jesus.

I am a chaplain for a local police department, and I was trained under my senior chaplain, Todd Pynch. The first six months of training, he simply instructed me to stay close to him, to say nothing, and to remember everything he did. That is what following Jesus looks like. Jesus wants us to stay close to His side, say nothing unless instructed, and remember everything He does.

We live in a culture that is forever talking, not listening. We live in a culture that, when it gets bored with one thing, moves on to the next bit of excitement. We live in a culture that doesn't want to remember history because it is not relevant to life—*wrong!* Jesus wants us to remember what He tells us and what He shows us. Take off your backpack and put away your phone! Jesus is about to teach you something.

Gospel Grit Challenge: Are you listening to Jesus? Are you staying close to Jesus? Can you smell Jesus? (This is an indicator of how close to Him you are really walking. He spends a lot of time with sheep; shepherds are that way. Sheep stink.) Try to remember the things He has taught you and the things He has shown you. Share some of those findings with others.

S—MATTHEW 8:16: "HE CAST OUT DEMONS AND HEALED ALL WHO WERE SICK."

(See also Matthew 8:32, Matthew 9:33, Matthew 10:1, Matthew 15:28, Matthew 17:18, Mark 1:25, Mark 1:34, Mark 3:14–15, Mark 5:8, Mark 5:30, Mark 7:29, Mark 9:25, Luke 4:35, Luke 4:40–41, Luke 7:21, Luke 8:33, Luke 8:39, Luke 9:1–2, Luke 10:19–20, and Luke 11:14; twenty-one references.)

I have referenced this verse under healing as well, but I wanted to discuss it on its own because I did not want to lose the demon piece of this verse or the twenty other references to casting out demons in the Gospels. This is a strange subject for many Christians. Considering Jesus cast out so many demons, where are all the demons today? Did He get rid of all of them and run them out of town for the next twenty centuries? Are they all in Africa? Perhaps they are as numerous today as they were in Jesus's day, and we cannot recognize them. Perhaps we are ignoring them. Perhaps they are everywhere and Christians are oblivious to them.

I have been involved in four specific situations that involved casting out demons. I do not wish this event on anyone. It was hair-raising. It was spiritual warfare. It was a battle between good and evil, God and Satan.

I have always understood that in situations involving demon possession, someone should be praying, someone should be reading Scripture, and someone should be casting out the demon. This was the case in three of the four situations I was in. Each ended with the demon being cast out. The fourth incident was much different than the other three, as I was not directly involved from start to finish with the event.

Jesus is showing us demons in the Gospels and what to do with them. He is preparing us for what we will be doing as followers of Jesus Christ. This isn't for everyone. Yet everyone needs to know about this subject. At the very least, Christians need to be aware so they can pray. Christians need to be aware so they can be informed as to what really is going on in spiritual warfare. Christians need to be aware because Jesus made this a major portion of the Gospels! If it is important to Jesus, it needs to be important to us.

Gospel Grit Challenge: Are you aware of demons? What can you specifically do to take part in this aspect of spiritual warfare? What more do you need to know about demons to be better prepared?

S—MATTHEW 8:18: "HE SAW THE CROWD AND GAVE ORDERS TO DEPART TO THE OTHER SIDE."

(See also Matthew 9:36, Matthew 14:22, Matthew 15:39, Mark 7:17, John 4:6, and John 6:5; seven references.)

Jesus was with crowds and with individuals. He was with small groups and large groups. I contend that if you are doing anything worthwhile, a crowd will eventually follow. Imagine if Jesus had had access to the Internet, social media networks, television, radio, and whatever else is available today. He would have been the most viral person of His day! He would have been the star of every YouTube video on the Internet. Can you imagine the feeding of the five thousand on the Internet? Would He have lasted three years in our day? Would He have died on a cross? Jesus found a way to be relevant in His day, and as we follow Him, He will help us to be relevant for our day.

You and I may not draw large crowds like Jesus did, but whoever

God gives us is the crowd He chooses for us to influence toward Him. My encouragement to all of us is to recognize the groups we find ourselves in from day to day and know this is "our crowd" for "our day" in order that we might lead people to Jesus. A very important part of following Jesus is to hand the baton to others, to give them a chance to run with Him too. It only makes sense that what we enjoy, we want others to enjoy too! Pull the baton out of your backpack and hand it to someone else to share in the race with you.

Gospel Grit Challenge: Who do you think you have influence over? Are you representing Jesus well? Where could you make improvements?

S—MATTHEW 8:24: "HE WAS ASLEEP IN THE BOAT IN A STORM."

(See also Matthew 8:34, Matthew 14:13, Matthew 16:4, Mark 3:7, Mark 3:20, Mark 4:36, Mark 6:31, Mark 7:33, Mark 8:13, Luke 4:42, John 5:13, John 6:15, and John 12:36; fourteen references.)

One of the priceless components of this study for me is seeing things I would not see in any other format. This verse and the thirteen that accompany it emphasize Jesus's being alone. I really did not realize how often Jesus slipped away from people just to be alone until I compiled this book. Jesus was really human. We can relate to that, can't we? There are times when it is great being with people, and there are other times when it is even greater not to be with people.

I love being with people. Being with people is a part of being a pastor, or at least it should be. But as much as I love being with people, when it is time to go home, I want to be alone—I mean really alone. I am glad Jesus took time to be alone. He did it for more than one reason, as you will see in the verses recorded above. It appears that some of the time, He just needed to take a break.

On the other hand, I always thought Jesus came to be with people, to help, to heal, to save, and to do all the other good He did. When I read of the passages where He wanted to get away from it all, at first it was confusing. It seemed that was time wasted when He could have been helping people. On the other hand, Jesus was not only thinking of the people of His day, He was setting an example for His followers for all days.

The takeaway for us can be this: if Jesus needed to take a break, so do we! If you thrive on being with people, I would encourage you to feed your own soul so you have something to give to others. Burnout can come when we fail to spend time alone recharging our batteries.

Gospel Grit Challenge: How much time do you need alone versus time with people? Are you giving enough alone time to yourself, not for the purpose of being selfish but for the purpose of being at your very best for others?

T—MATTHEW 8:26: "HE REBUKED THE WIND AND IT BECAME PERFECTLY CALM."

(See also Matthew 14:28, Mark 4:38, Mark 4:39, Mark 6:48, and John 6:19; six references.)

Jesus was always using His surroundings as teaching points, especially with the parables. Jesus used dirt and His finger to teach a lesson to the religious leaders and to set free a woman trapped in her sin. Jesus used food, as we will see a bit later in this study. Jesus used something as simple as water. Jesus used weather. Jesus is now using the sea as a tool for His power.

Think of the things in life that God has used to demonstrate His power to you. Take a look around you and look for ways God could be speaking to you and others. It is not that God is not speaking; it's that we are preoccupied.

Think of it: Jesus gets on a boat, a storm arises, and Jesus tells the sea to be calm as if it were a five-gallon bucket of water. For me, the power of God is demonstrated often through weather. I love going to the ocean. I love fishing off the beach and catching perch. (Perch are the most common fish to catch off the Oregon beaches, at least for me.) It is especially fun when you can get two on the line at the same time!

I also love going to the beach when it is stormy, because the power of the ocean is magnificent. On the central Oregon coast, there is a small drive-through town called Depoe Bay. When a really bad storm is brewing, waves can climb over the town's seawall. When I see this, I am amazed more than ever at the power in those waves. It is breathtakingly awesome!

Let's look for ways God can demonstrate His power in our lives. First, if we are experiencing a storm, know that Jesus is able to calm the storms of life just as easily as the storm on the sea. Second, if we are fearful of the waves of grief, or discouragement, or disappointment, or depression overpowering our souls, remember that we know the Master of the wind. Because He has calmed the physical weather, we know He can calm the spiritual storms of life. Third, the power in the waves is puny compared to the power of the Holy Spirit in our lives! The next time you experience a storm or watch the latest hurricane on television, let it be a reminder to you not of the destruction of the storm, but rather of the power of God in your life.

Gospel Grit Challenge: When you are in the storms of life, do you ask God to take away the storm or to keep you safe? How big is your God? Describe Him at work in your life.

S—MATTHEW 9:10: "JESUS DINED WITH MANY SINNERS."

(See also Matthew 14:19, Matthew 15:36, Matthew 21:18, Matthew 26:26–29, Mark 2:15, Mark 6:37, Mark 6:41, Mark 8:2, Mark 8:6, Mark 8:7, Mark 11:12, Mark 14:22, Mark 14:23, Luke 7:36, Luke 9:16, Luke 22:17, Luke 22:19, Luke 24:30, Luke 24:42–43, John 2:1–11, John 4:7, John 4:32, John 6:11, John 6:12, John 6:27, John 6:51, John 6:58, John 7:10, John 7:37–38, John 19:28, John 21:6, John 21:10, and John 21:12; thirty-four references.)

I am so glad Jesus was fully God and *fully human*. Can you imagine how hollow the Gospels would be if we were to take out all of the references to food? Food and water are basic to sustaining life.

I have been a pastor now for thirty-three years. I have sat through, have taught, and have participated in almost every version of evangelism there is. Jesus is teaching all of us Evangelism 101 in the Gospels. Food appears to be a great way to win people over to Jesus. It works in the business world, so why shouldn't it work in evangelism? It has been said that educators take a simple truth and make it difficult, while a communicator takes a difficult truth and makes it simple. Do you get the idea that Jesus is on to something here? When He went to the tax collector's house, His excuse to get in the door was dinner. Even enemies of the cross have to eat!

In the list of Scriptures above, I have referenced times when Jesus was thirsty as well. This list is a good reminder to us that Jesus was bound by a human body just as we are. Jesus set the world on fire in three short years. Our task as His followers is to stir the coals and to fan the flames of the gospel.

Gospel Grit Challenge: Who should you share a meal with for the sake of the gospel?

T—MATTHEW 9:13: "GO AND LEARN WHAT THIS MEANS."

I grew up a typical boy who wanted to do anything but be in school. We lived on a wonderful property with woods enough to shoot a BB gun and a field out front to play baseball and hit golf balls. It was a marvelous place to be raised. The only drawback was school. I had some problems learning, as some things did not come easily for me.

When I got to college school still was not easy, but now it was costing a lot of money so I knew I had better do my best. But knowing isn't necessarily doing—I really did not do my best and consequently did not learn as much as I could have. Seminary was not much different, as now

I was married and just wanted to have a job at a church. School took a backseat yet again.

It wasn't until my doctoral program that I really applied myself to my studies and took in every word like a sponge thirsty for water. It was at that junction that I realized I had wasted some golden opportunities in life, but I was determined to do better in the future.

When Jesus tells us to learn something, I believe He wants us to give it 100 percent. There is so much for us to learn from Him, I wonder if we sometimes miss golden opportunities to sit at the feet of Professor Jesus.

Last year I spoke at the college where I am an adjunct professor and shared with the students ten thoughts I wish, now that I am fifty, that I had known at twenty.

1. Spiritual warfare is real.
2. The years between twenty and fifty go by really fast.
3. If you marry, invest everything you have into it.
4. All jobs are a ministry.
5. Spend more time in the Scripture.
6. Do everything in light of eternity
7. People die.
8. Save more so you can give more.
9. Lead more people to Christ.
10. Keep learning.

Gospel Grit Challenge: What do you think God is trying to teach you in the season of life you find yourself in? Are you willing to learn new truths from God? What is the last new truth you learned from God?

S—MATTHEW 9:25: "JESUS BROUGHT A DEAD GIRL BACK TO LIFE."

(See also Matthew 10:28, Matthew 16:21, Matthew 27:50, Mark 14:34, Mark 15:37, Luke 8:55, Luke 9:60, Luke 12:4, John 3:16, John 5:24, John 6:53–54,

John 8:24, John 8:51, John 11:5, John 11:25, John 11:33, John 11:35, John 11:38, John 11:43–44, John 19:30, and John 19:34; twenty-two references.)

As we study the Gospels, we can see every aspect of human life from miracles to preaching to laughter to eating and sleeping. So we must include the subject of death. Death is a subject most everyone would like to avoid, especially when it is our own death. Yet death is unavoidable.

I recently visited our state penitentiary in Oregon and was permitted to visit death row, a place few are allowed to go. I was allowed to view the death chamber as well, a place even fewer people are allowed to see. As I left the facility that hot Thursday afternoon, it dawned on me that we all are on death row! None of us are getting out of here alive. It kind of makes you wish you had taken Bob's comments on Death Therapy in the movie *What About Bob?* more seriously, doesn't it? Jesus is actually teaching us about Death Therapy in these passages.

As much as we try to prepare for death, we are never fully prepared for it. We can plan and plot and do our best, but when that moment comes, it is like the Twin Towers imploding in our hearts.

You will note I included John 3:16 in the above list. I could have included it in many lists in this study. I chose to group it under the topic of death because the very essence of eternal life is salvation from eternal death. It sounds obvious, yet I believe it to be quite profound. We learn from Jesus that our last breath on earth gives way to our first breath in heaven. Think of the hope that is ours as followers of Jesus Christ.

Gospel Grit Challenge: Are you saved, born again, a follower of Jesus Christ? If yes, then shout. If no, is there any reason why right now would not be a great time to bow your head and ask Jesus to forgive you of your sins? Will you take this time to receive Jesus into your heart and life and trust Him with your future? (If you just received Jesus into your life, I would love to hear from you. Please find my contact information in the back of this book.)

T—MATTHEW 9:38: "BESEECH THE LORD OF THE HARVEST TO SEND OUT WORKERS INTO HIS HARVEST."

(See also Matthew 10:5–6, Matthew 10:22, Matthew 10:32, Matthew 10:33, Matthew 10:39, Matthew 11:20, Matthew 15:24, Matthew 18:11, Matthew 19:29, Matthew 20:28, Matthew 24:13, Mark 1:15, Mark 2:17, Mark 13:13, Mark 16:15, Luke 9:24, Luke 9:56, Luke 13:3, Luke 13:5, Luke 14:13, Luke 15:7, Luke 17:33, Luke 19:5, Luke 19:10, Luke 23:43, Luke 24:25, and Luke 24:47; twenty-eight references.)

Based on repetition, we can see about a dozen primary themes in the Gospels. Salvation is certainly at the top of that list. There is much discussion on which is more important: the chicken or the egg. It used to matter which came first. Now what matters is what is most important. There are Christian leaders arguing for social justice over salvation, and I dare say in place of personal salvation. Social justice is important in the Gospels, yet salvation is premier!

It is interesting to note that when we stand before God, and we will, we will not stand with others. According to all the passages in the Bible that address this event, we will stand alone. It makes sense then that salvation is personal.

It is likewise true that we will stand before God on judgment day and give an account of the deeds done in the body, good deeds and bad. This is where division has barged into the church. There are some people arguing for social justice as primary, while there is nobody arguing for salvation only as important. An important part of being a Christian is helping the oppressed, but helping the oppressed does not necessarily lead to salvation.

Everyone has his or her opinion. I have mine. I believe salvation comes first and our deeds to those in need follow. Jesus died on the cross for the poverty of my soul, not for the poverty of my checkbook. Jesus died for my sins, not my financial position.

Jesus made salvation a priority, and so should we as His followers. The relationship of salvation and social justice is a both-and proposition, not an either-or. Salvation comes first and is most important.

Gospel Grit Challenge: When was the last time you shared the plan of salvation with someone? Name the person you last led to the Lord.

Passing out coffee under the bridge is easy and no substitute for sharing salvation with people. Remember, these are Gospel Grit challenges. Jesus never said following Him would be easy!

S—MATTHEW 10:11: "HE TOLD THE TWELVE THAT WHEN THEY ARRIVED AT A CITY, THEY WERE TO INQUIRE WHO IS WORTHY IN A CITY TO STAY THERE."

(See also Matthew 14:25, Mark 3:13, Mark 4:34, Mark 8:27, Mark 8:29, Mark 8:30, Mark 10:32, Mark 14:17, Luke 6:13, Luke 8:23, Luke 8:24, Luke 9:10, Luke 18:31, John 3:22, John 4:2, John 6:3, John 11:54, John 13:5, John 21:1; twenty references.)

They would arrive at a village with backpacks in tow, dirty, dusty, and probably dripping with sweat. In the Wild West they would have been known as a posse. On the streets of Harlem they would be called a gang. On the field they would be called a team. To Jesus, they were His disciples. Imagine having twelve guys follow you just about everywhere you went for three grueling years. That fact alone would have driven me nuts! No wonder Jesus wanted to be alone from time to time.

Have you ever wondered why twelve? Perhaps Jesus chose twelve disciples to represent the twelve tribes of Israel. Perhaps Jesus chose twelve because He needed that many to pick up the baskets of food after the feeding of the masses. Perhaps Jesus chose twelve knowing how many bases would need to be covered after He split the scene. Whatever the reason, the number sure seemed to be important to Jesus, because when Judas checked out, he was replaced.

They certainly were not the most educated. They certainly were not the most polite. They certainly were not the most religious. They didn't even represent all walks of life. Yet, when they met Jesus, every single one of them left everything they were doing and followed Him for three years. Much of the time they were not even sure if He was the real deal. They grumbled and complained at times. They doubted at times. They fell asleep when they were supposed to be awake. They vanished when times got tough for Jesus. Yet in the end they followed Jesus, and most all of them ended up dying a martyr's death. Praise God for the twelve!

Gospel Grit Challenge: What do you have to offer Jesus should He need another twelve? Would you follow Him all the way to your death? Actually, we have been called to follow. On a scale of 1–10, with 10 being perfect, how well are you following Jesus? If you are at a 6, what can you do differently in the next six months to make that a 7? What steps can you take to keep raising that number?

T—MATTHEW 10:12: "AS YOU ENTER THE HOUSE, GIVE IT YOUR GREETING."

This instruction is more significant than first meets the eye. Jesus is teaching us something much deeper than just door-to-door evangelism. Jesus is telling us to give every person in this world the benefit of the doubt. Of course, if something goes wrong that changes things, but always start by giving people a chance.

This sounds easy until we run across a difficult character. Jesus is telling us to be kind and gracious and warm and friendly. This is an important part in being a follower of Jesus. We must remember whom we represent.

I never have been fond of putting our church name on our church vehicles. Many do it for advertising. I shy away from it. If you have ever been a youth pastor, and I have, you know exactly what I am talking about. You can have the strictest rules in the world, and before you know it a precious youth does something not very precious. Guess who gets called into the senior pastor's office after getting a call from a driver who took down the number from the side of the vehicle? Wherever we go, we represent Jesus.

Gospel Grit Challenge: Are you kind and warm and friendly? Do you

*give people the benefit of the doubt before jumping to conclusions about
them or rejecting them? How can you improve on the "warm fuzzies"
to be more like Jesus with people you meet?*

T—MATTHEW 10:14: "WHOEVER DOES NOT RECEIVE YOU…SHAKE THE
DUST OFF YOUR FEET."

(See also Mark 6:10–11; two references.)

Rejection. What an awful experience. It happens all throughout life.
It happens with athletics, it happens in the workplace, it happens in relationships. Rejection is a very painful part of life. People like myself try
very hard to succeed just because the fear of rejection is so painful.

Jesus is teaching His followers that not everyone is going to appre-
ciate the message they deliver. I love this about Jesus: He says to just
shake the rejection off and keep right on trucking! The reality of the
gospel is, some are going to like it and others are going to despise it. This
is not your problem or mine; it belongs to God. Jesus is telling us not to
take it personally. This is a hard lesson to learn; nonetheless, it is valuable
to grasp.

*Gospel Grit Challenge: Who has rejected you in your church? Forgive.
Who has rejected you in a relationship? Forgive. Who has rejected
you in life? Forgive and move on.*

T—MATTHEW 10:16: "BE SHREWD AS SERPENTS AND INNOCENT AS
DOVES."

---

*(See also Matthew 10:17, Matthew 24:42, Matthew 24:44, Matthew 25:13,
Mark 13:9, Mark 13:23, Mark 13:33, Mark 13:35, Mark 13:37, Luke 12:35,
Luke 12:40, Luke 21:8, and Luke 21:36; fourteen references.)*

The number of times Jesus cautions us to be alert in the Gospels is
significant. Christians are many times oblivious to their surroundings

and to spiritual warfare. We are often guilty of being naïve, assuming things are better than they really are.

Jesus is telling us to be alert to many things. Most importantly, He wants us to be alert to His return. He wants us to be ready. This is what being a follower of Jesus Christ is about. Readiness means being prepared to seize the opportunities before us on His behalf.

Truthfully, we can get caught up in this life to the extent that we lose sight of His return. The pessimist would believe that because Jesus has waited for two thousand years, He could easily delay His return for two thousand more years. That may be true. However, we will not live that long, so it is best for you and me to be as ready as possible for His return! The more closely we follow Him, the more ready we will be.

Jesus is also telling us to be on the alert for those who would deceive us. There are many people who prey on Christians. They are evil and greedy and malicious. How many times have innocent, trusting people given money to another "Christian" who wants to invest their money, guaranteeing a handsome return on their investment? I know of one elderly couple in our church who gave their entire life savings for such a promise. The ending was predictable: they lost it all. Jesus tells us to be on the alert.

Jesus is telling us to be on the alert for people who would lead us astray spiritually too. How is it so many Christians get sucked into such schemes? One answer would be that we are not grounded in the Scriptures. Another answer would be that we are not grounded in the Scriptures. And yet another answer might be that we are not grounded in the Scriptures! And then there is the whole subject of false teaching which Jesus addresses elsewhere.

We fail to use discernment. This word is used thirty-eight times in the Bible. That is enough repetition to understand how important it is to be discerning. To discern is to know the difference between truth and falsehood, to know the difference between right and wrong, to know the difference between good and evil. It is shocking to note how many people lack discernment.

We must look out for one another because the enemy can creep into our midst and pull people away one by one, and before we know it, damage has been done. Jesus tells us to be on the alert because we live in a sick, twisted, demented world.

As we strive to show the world our love for God, Jesus is telling us to pray with one eye open!

Gospel Grit Challenge: Have you ever been spiritually confused? How do you go about bringing clarity into your spiritual life? Are you thinking daily in terms of alertness, or have you set your weapon down? As a hunter, the moment I set my weapon down, that is when the trophy walks by and I am unprepared. As Christians, it isn't a trophy passing our way, it is our enemy, Satan! Be on the alert!

T—MATTHEW 10:20: "IT IS NOT YOU WHO SPEAK, IT IS THE SPIRIT OF YOUR FATHER WHO SPEAKS IN YOU."

(See also Matthew 12:31, Matthew 28:19–20, Mark 3:11, Mark 3:29, Luke 4:14, Luke 10:21, Luke 12:11–12, Luke 24:49, and John 20:22; ten references.)

Jesus was fully God, yet fully human. Like us, He too needed to be clothed with power from heaven. What is this power? It is a person, the third person of the Holy Trinity: the Holy Spirit.

Please note that Jesus did not begin His formal ministry, which included miracles and manifestations of God's power, until He had received the Holy Spirit. If Jesus needed the Holy Spirit, we need the Holy Spirit.

Jesus tells us the Holy Spirit will guide us into all truth. He declares the Holy Spirit will convict the world of sin and righteousness and judgment and the things that are to come. Jesus tells us the Holy Spirit will be our Comforter.

I absolutely love the months of September and October in the Willamette Valley. I do not know of two months that are more beautiful anywhere in the world. The days are warm but not hot. The nights are cool but not cold. The leaves begin to change, and the wind begins to blow. The Willamette Valley is located sixty miles from the Pacific Ocean. I love the first storm of the season, which usually blows into our area sometime in October. The sun has gone down, the window is open, the wind is blowing, the rain is pelting down, the trees are howling, and I am in bed under my nice warm comforter taking it all in.

When the storms of life come, and they will, we have a Comforter we can find warmth and security under. He will guide us into all truth. And because Jesus is Truth, the Holy Spirit will lead us directly to Jesus.

We know that Jesus ascended to the Father shortly after the story of the Gospels, but not before promising us the presence of the Holy Spirit. If Jesus is the steak, the Holy Spirit is the crème brulee! I have a friend who, on a cruise one night, ordered all eight desserts on the menu. We laughed and laughed, but for her it was serious business. She loves dessert. Following Jesus leads us to the dessert of Christianity: the Holy Spirit.

Gospel Grit challenge: How well do you know the Holy Spirit? What is the Holy Spirit doing in your life right now? Do you need to be filled with the Holy Spirit? Have you been empowered by the Holy Spirit? Do you sense His presence in your life?

T—MATTHEW 10:26: "DO NOT FEAR THEM."

(See also Matthew 10:31, Matthew 14:27, Matthew 17:7, Matthew 24:6, Matthew 28:10, Mark 5:36, Mark 6:50, Mark 13:7, Luke 5:10, Luke 12:7, Luke 12:32, Luke 21:9, John 6:20, and John 14:27; fifteen references.)

Most people fear something, and often more than one thing. Some people, especially children, fear the darkness. Some people fear snakes and spiders and rats. Some people fear losing their job. Some people fear relationships. Some people fear dying. Some people fear never having enough money. Some people fear the future. Some people fear strangers, while others fear those closest to them. Some people fear heights. Some people fear flying. Some people fear cancer. The list is endless.

Jesus teaches us to not fear. This is easier said than done if the fear within is real. How do we move from fear to faith? The whole point of discipleship is to be close to Jesus in a covenant relationship. It is not a contractual relationship; it is a covenantal relationship. We must find ways to follow closely to Jesus. We need to be close enough to Him so that we can see the zippers on His backpack. We need to follow so close to Him that we can see the sweat on the back of His neck from a Middle Eastern sun.

The key to conquering fear is a relationship with Jesus Christ. For years I have heard people speak of the importance of marrying another Christian. While I agree with this, it falls far short of the mark. The question must be asked, "What kind of a relationship does one have with Jesus?" We all know Christians who hardly could pick Jesus out of a lineup, while others live at His feet. Jesus is instructing His followers to live at His feet. The closer we are to Him, the less we will fear; He guarantees it!

Gospel Grit Challenge: Name your fears. Define your closeness to Jesus Christ. In what ways can you live closer to Him, starting today?

T—MATTHEW 10:27: "WHAT I TELL YOU IN THE DARKNESS, SPEAK IN THE LIGHT; AND WHAT YOU HEAR WHISPERED IN YOUR EAR, PROCLAIM AMONG THE HOUSETOPS."

One of the greatest things about knowing Jesus is the personal relationship we enter into, a relationship that is wonderfully real. He speaks to us primarily in Scripture. There are also those moments when, in our prayer closet or in the grocery store, we hear from Jesus. I have discovered that He most often speaks to me when I am alone. I have likewise discovered that I have to be still, because He has never shouted at me. He uses that low-toned voice like Jack Bauer on *24*, the action-packed show that played for a few years.

Jesus is constantly sending us text messages. He wants us to post them on our Facebook so the whole world may know of His great love.

Have you ever watched a Japanese salesman in training? I have watched specials on cable showing them yelling at the top of their lungs on a busy street corner. The purpose is to give them boldness to sell products without fear of what others think. This is exactly where we need to be with the message of Jesus Christ.

Christians have been boxed into the corner of political correctness and smothered with a blanket of tolerance. It has caused the message of Jesus Christ to be compromised and at times silenced. Jesus is instructing us to take what is given us in secret and share it with great boldness until the whole world has heard the good news.

Gospel Grit Challenge: How has political correctness altered your Christianity? How has tolerance altered your Christianity? Are you impacting culture with the gospel, or is culture impacting you with its message? Think this one through.

T—MATTHEW 10:34: "I DID NOT COME TO BRING PEACE, BUT A SWORD."

Wow! What are we going to do with this teaching? Are we supposed to take up weapons and start a war? Let's try to consider what Jesus is telling us given the whole of the Gospels. God is love. God offers us peace and tells us not to fight. So what could Jesus mean by this teaching?

Jesus came to change the religious order of the day because it was broken. It wasn't working, at least in the opinion of God! Jesus came to bring about a reformation, a revolution. Jesus came to fix what was broken—us!

Whenever change is in the air, so is resistance. We are creatures of habit. I had a roommate in college who made it his goal to never change the sheets on his bed for an entire term. He was successful, at my expense. He played basketball most nights, came in late, and lay down on his sheets with his stinky, sweaty body. It was gross. What began as white sheets over the course of the term slowly turned to a light gray and then a dirty brown. (Of course, I don't think my friend was opposed to change so much as he was too lazy to change his bedding.)

Christians, like most people, do not like a lot of change; thus many churches are dead and in full denial over it. Further, some are lazy and do not want to put forth the effort Jesus demands. Jesus came to bring about transformation, reformation, a revolution! We approach Christianity some days as if it is a picnic. It is not! Eternity is at stake! Wake up, Church! Wake up, Christian!

Following Jesus Christ demands sacrifice and obedience. Following Jesus Christ demands intense fellowship. I have friends who are married, and when they argue they call it "intense fellowship." This is not what I am referring to. I am referencing a relationship with Jesus that is alive, active, and, as the opening theme from Star Trek states, is "boldly going where no man has gone before." This is following Jesus Christ.

Did you notice that early on in the Gospels, Jesus asked us to forgive everyone we do not like and give away just about everything we own? (See Matthew 5.) He is asking us to strap on a backpack and trust Him fully!

Gospel Grit Challenge: Is Christianity boring for you? Have you ever been on a foreign mission trip with your church? Have you ever visited a jail and explored ways to reach out to prisoners? Christianity can be exciting if you are willing to leave your couch and turn off the stupid television set. What is Jesus asking you to change in order to follow Him?

T—MATTHEW 11:25: "I PRAISE YOU, FATHER."

If Jesus praises the Father, so should I. Praise is acknowledging His greatness. Praise to the Father helps us to stop praising ourselves! We live in a very selfish culture. We are constantly praising our own efforts. Politicians are notorious for this. With fame, money, power, and success come praise. Like money, we must keep working at giving it away.

It has been a tradition in church in this country that the minister stands at the door after church is over to greet people. Usually the short-lived conversations are friendly, complimentary, and very uplifting. I recall one Sunday after I had concluded a communion service that I recall being extra meaningful, I was in the lobby saying good-bye to people. A man came over to me, leaned toward my ear, and said, "Do you actually think these people give a rat's *** what you just said?" I was stunned. I will never forget that moment or those words. Yet more damaging than someone saying hurtful words are those people who puff us up with mis-placed praise. We are fragile creatures. We need praise. Pastors need praise. In our cravings for praise, may we never forget who *deserves* the praise, credit, and glory for anything we may accomplish in this life: Jesus Christ. Praise is something that may well come your way and mine, but may we never forget who gave us such opportunities.

There are many ways to praise God. I attend a church with a con-gregation that comes from seventy-two identifiable church backgrounds (as identified by a survey I did in church one day). I grew up being taught to show little to no emotion in church. Today I freely raise my hands in praise to God. Praise to God does not require lifting hands or other out-ward actions, but it *does* require lifting our hearts in praise to God with our voices! This is a must.

Gospel Grit Challenge: Next time you go to church, praise God for your salvation. Next time you go to church, praise God for your eternal life. Next time you go to church, praise God for the forgiveness of sin. Next time you go to church, praise God for His peace. Next time you go to church, praise God for His greatness. Next time you go to church, praise God from whom all blessings flow. Next time you go to church, PRAISE THE FATHER!

T—MATTHEW 11:28–29: "COME TO ME, ALL WHO ARE WEARY AND HEAVY LADEN, AND I WILL GIVE YOU REST. TAKE MY YOKE UPON YOU AND LEARN FROM ME, FOR I AM GENTLE AND HUMBLE IN HEART, AND YOU WILL FIND REST FOR YOUR SOULS."

Jesus knows what He is talking about on this one. (Actually, He knows what He is talking about on all of them!) Remember, He is on a three-year hike through Israel with a backpack filled with heartache, burdens, sickness, and brokenness. Jesus is homeless and unemployed. These three years for Jesus are not easy. When He tells the weary and the heavy-laden to come to Him, He is actually asking people to join His support group. This could be the first recorded support group in Christianity. Who better to lead the group than the one who has the heaviest backpack!

Everybody needs rest. The youngest and the strongest need rest. Much of the time we live our lives on high octane, burning the candle at both ends. We live much of life worn out and burned out. Is it really worth it? Jesus comes along and tells us to take a break. He offers us something nobody else in this world can offer and deliver on: rest for the soul.

Part of following Jesus is going to school. It is not the typical course with the typical syllabus and the typical professor. Jesus is our guest professor. He resides in heaven. For a short time He came to earth so we could *learn* from Him. His syllabus does not include exams, quizzes, or term papers. His class is all about life and living it abundantly. Jesus knew this world would take its toll on us. He knew our backpacks would get heavy in certain seasons. As a student, I greatly disliked certain parts of my courses. As a professor, I have attempted to make life more fruitful for my students than my professors did for me. Jesus is determined that we will all pass. In order to pass His course, we must take time to rest our souls in His care. Following Him is all about doing life with Him, not doing it alone!

Gospel Grit Challenge: What is weighing you down? What do you need to take out of your backpack and give to Jesus right now? Rest, rejuvenate, relax, chill, smell the roses, look up!

T—MATTHEW 12:30: "HE WHO IS NOT WITH ME IS AGAINST ME; AND HE WHO DOES NOT GATHER WITH ME SCATTERS."

What kind of a person are you? Are you a person who lives life in moderation? Are you a person who is all-in? Is your cup half-full or half-empty? Jesus is telling us something very important about following Him. He is telling us that if we are going to be a Christian on Sunday and do something else Monday through Saturday, then we are not following Him at all.

Does that sound harsh? I know we need to leave room for growth. But we also need to know that if we are going to represent the King of Kings, we must know what is in His head and His heart. He is not asking for a 50 percent commitment. He is not asking for a 75 percent commitment. He is not asking for a 99 percent commitment. He is asking for 100 percent. Either we are following Him or we are not.

Neutral is not found in the Gospels. Neutral is vanilla. Jesus is looking for people who will pick up His cross and follow Him to places that are not popular. Jesus is telling us to follow Him, and that means to give 100 percent all of the time.

I do not wake up some mornings thinking I am going to give Jesus 81 percent. That is not how a follower of Jesus Christ thinks. I wake up thinking I want to follow Him wherever He may lead me. Life is an adventure with Jesus. He will take you down trails you did not know existed in this world outside of knowing Him. He likewise will be with you during trials you do not think you can survive. Follow Him!

Gospel Grit Challenge: What holds you back from giving Him everything? Who is influencing you, if anybody, to give Jesus less than 100 percent of your life?

T—MATTHEW 12:37: "BY YOUR WORDS YOU WILL BE JUSTIFIED, AND BY YOUR WORDS YOU WILL BE CONDEMNED."

Words matter. Many of us grew up being taught the saying, "Sticks and stones may break my bones, but names will never hurt me." Strangely (or not-so-strangely), it was just the opposite in my life. I grew up never being hurt once by a stick or a stone, yet was bloodied up many times by words!

Jesus is telling us to make our words count. Jesus is telling us our words will either do a lot of good or a lot of harm. Words matter because the Bible matters. I recognize that we live in an image-driven society today, but that does not negate the necessity of words.

Jesus is telling us to make our words the kind of words that will set us free, not put us in chains. Words can free, or they can put in bondage. This applies to others as well. We have an opportunity to either build people up or to tear people down.

Following Jesus includes what we do with our mouths. This has something to do with what is in our heads and our hearts. If we will apply the other truths taught by Jesus about following Him, this one will take care of itself. My encouragement to you is to follow Jesus the person and follow the words of Jesus as well. If we have His heart, we will begin to speak His words. It is a beautiful thing to experience. It is all a part of following Jesus.

Gospel Grit Challenge: Is there anything in your backpack that would cause you to speak poorly spoken words? Think of positive ways you can generate words that will set you free rather than words that will tie you up. Words are a result of what is in the head and the heart. When was the last time you checked under the hood?

T—MATTHEW 13:12: "FOR WHOEVER HAS, TO HIM SHALL MORE BE GIVEN, AND HE WILL HAVE AN ABUNDANCE; BUT WHOEVER DOES NOT HAVE, EVEN WHAT HE HAS SHALL BE TAKEN FROM HIM."

This statement is hardly support for socialism! Jesus is teaching us a priceless principle of responsibility, accountability, integrity, and opportunity. Jesus wants us to bear fruit. It really is that simple. How we handle what we have now affects how much we can grow in the future.

We can be very busy in the orchard and never bear fruit. I have a friend in the church who owns a cherry orchard. His fruit each year is marvelous, and I get to enjoy a small sack each harvest. He spends the entire year preparing the trees so that when nature does its thing, the trees will have every possible advantage needed to bear a bumper crop. Jesus is not teaching us to be busy; Jesus is teaching us to be productive!

This verse has much to do with gifts and abilities too. Chances are, the person who worked his tail off has much and can handle more. The one who has not worked for it probably would not want it anyway.

For those struggling with fairness and equity, Jesus is clearly teaching us something about these things too: life is not fair, and equal distribution is not God's way. Some people were just created to take care of other people.

Gospel Grit Challenge: What has God placed in your care? Are you using your gifts and talents? Are you making the most of your time or wasting it? What can you change right now to be a better follower of Jesus in this area?

T—MATTHEW 13:16: "BLESSED ARE YOUR EYES, BECAUSE THEY SEE; AND YOUR EARS, BECAUSE THEY HEAR."

One evening when I was watching Monday night football early in my marriage, my wife was talking to me and I did not hear a word she said. She made several attempts (or so she said) to get my attention. She eventually got my attention when she turned off the television set. By the way, I no longer watch Monday night football!

How many times do we sit in church but do not hear and see? How many times are we preoccupied and miss something important God is telling us? How many times does God make Himself known, yet we are busy watching something else?

"Blessed" is a great thing to be and to experience. God wants to bless us. However, we must be good listeners and fix both our eyes and our ears on Jesus. This is why following Jesus is so very important. When we are following *closely*, we will have better opportunity to hear His voice and see what He is showing us.

Most of us come into this world fairly blind and deaf. The Holy Spirit is our bifocals, and the Holy Spirit is our hearing aid. To be in tune with Jesus, we need to be in tune with the Holy Spirit. To be in tune with the Holy Spirit, we need to be following *close* to Jesus.

Following Jesus is not about following from a distance; rather, it is about being as close as possible so we can hear and see, up close and personal, what He is communicating. When going to a ball game, the tickets that cost the most are the seats closest to the action. Jesus has invited us to the front row. He wants us to hear everything He has to say and see everything He wants to show us!

Gospel Grit Challenge: How often do you see Jesus at work in your life? How often do you hear His voice? How can you open your eyes and ears wider?

S—MATTHEW 13:58: "HE DID NOT DO MANY MIRACLES THERE BECAUSE OF THEIR UNBELIEF."

Let's apply this teaching to the average church service. Many people would say church is boring. According to some, there are roughly 3,500 churches closing in America per year. Roughly two million people are leaving the church annually. Would this be happening if miracles were happening in our midst? Of course not! It seems to me the church is in need of Jesus showing up. But how is this going to happen?

I believe that the vast majority of Scripture is intended to be taken literally. I believe that what Jesus said is what Jesus meant. I believe He stated it literally so we would not have to guess what He meant. Remember what I said a few pages ago: words matter.

A wise rule to follow would be to emulate the example of the one in the Gospels who proclaimed his belief and asked God to change his unbelief. In fact, I think this Sunday when I preach, I am going to do this at the beginning of my message. I might even enjoy church this Sunday if God shows up!

We are voiding ourselves of God's best for us because we fail to to take Him at His Word. Just believe. Only believe. Believe. Don't doubt. Don't question. Don't search for the entire *why* of God. Believe!

Gospel Grit Challenge: What are your doubts about Jesus? What doesn't make sense? What doesn't add up? Believe!

S—MATTHEW 14:31: "IMMEDIATELY, JESUS STRETCHED OUT HIS HAND AND TOOK HOLD OF HIM."

I have always loved this verse, for two reasons. First, the picture of Jesus stretching out His hand to rescue me from drowning is powerful.

For approximately twenty-five years I worked with teenagers at a youth camp each summer. In the early years we were young and crazy and had lots of energy. On one occasion down at the dock on the edge of the lake, my friend brought a Lab puppy. Rosie decided to do what all Labs do, which is to jump into the water. Her problem was, probably due to the cold water, she began to sink. I quickly lay on the dock, reached down under the water, and grabbed her by the collar to pull her to safety. This is the image I get of Jesus taking care of me. I hope it is the image you get of Him taking care of you!

Second, this passage teaches us something about the importance of being in a place where we need Jesus. When you just sit on the shore, there really is no need for Jesus. You need Jesus when you push away from the dock and set sail for the deep waters. Something is bound to go wrong out there, and we know from this passage of Scripture that Jesus is there to snatch us up out of the water.

I have a friend who attends the church I pastor. He is a sailor and does charters out of Depoe Bay, Oregon. One day two friends and I went over to catch some fresh salmon out of the ocean. Before we pushed off, one of my friends was green and feeding the fish, if you know what I mean.

It was a cold, damp, and extremely foggy day. Once we were out in the ocean, the fog set in like a nasty growth on an old bottle of ketchup. I became so sick from the motion of the water that I could not have cared less about fishing. There was nothing in my backpack that was attractive in that situation. I needed rescuing. It wasn't my friend's fault. He did everything he could to help me. I was beyond rescuing.

In the sea of life, nobody is outside of the reach of Jesus, especially when we are following Him closely. My advice to you is to stay within arm's length of Jesus. That should give you all the insurance, assurance, and protection needed should the fog set in upon your life.

Gospel Grit Challenge: Are you living life in the fog right now? Jesus is closer than you think! Don't give up on following Jesus. Bad circumstances do not mean He is far away; it means He is within arm's length of your life. Hang in there!

T—MATTHEW 15:11: "IT IS NOT WHAT ENTERS INTO THE MOUTH THAT DEFILES THE MAN, BUT WHAT PROCEEDS OUT OF THE MOUTH, THIS DEFILES THE MAN."

(See also Mark 7:20; two references.)

Jesus is teaching us another priceless lesson about life here. While it is true that what comes out of our mouths causes all the trouble, that comes as a result of what we put into our mouths.

As a child I learned the song that said, "Be careful little eyes what you see, little ears what you hear, little feet where you go, little hands what you touch, little mouth what you say, because the Father up above is looking down in love." The Father is wanting me to follow His Son, Jesus, not the pleasures of this world. It is a children's song, but it seems to me it should be an adult song, given all the problems we seem to have as adults with these areas of our lives!

My wife is good about eating healthy food, or at least about telling me what I should eat. She is really smart in this area, and I know she is usually right. If I keep eating processed sugar, the outcome is inevitable. If I start eating more greens and vegetables, the outcome is just as inevitable. We are what we eat.

Spiritually, we are what we take into our souls. Jesus wants us to be cautious how we live because there is much at stake. If we are following Him but are eating the things of the world out of our backpacks, we will eventually stop following Him. It all goes back to asking, "What is in my backpack?"

Gospel Grit Challenge: Who or what influences you? Does this influence make you a better follower of Christ or not? Make changes if necessary.

T—MATTHEW 15:32: "I FEEL COMPASSION FOR THE PEOPLE."

(See also Mark 1:41, Mark 6:34, Luke 7:13, and Luke 22:51; five references.)

We should be so thankful for this tiny little teaching! If we eliminated compassion from Jesus's life, we would have to eliminate the cross, and we would be sunk without it. Compassion moves the world. Compassion changes the world. Compassion is a direct result of a transformed heart. Compassion is contagious. Compassion is something that is not only taught but caught. Jesus is teaching us to be compassionate, and He is also showing us what compassion looks like through the people He helped.

None of us are as good as Jesus; nonetheless, we can still have a pound of compassion in our backpack. Where compassion is lacking, selfishness abounds. Where selfishness is void, compassion abounds. It seems to be one or the other. Jesus definitely teaches us to be moved with compassion. Our desire to help others must grow as strong as our desire to help ourselves. This is the essence of compassion.

While there are only five passages that state Jesus's compassion for the people, we know from observation that the entirety of the Gospels is about compassion. Compassion comes from a heart that sees from God's eternal perspective.

Gospel Grit Challenge: Whom could you help today? Where is your compassion level? Following Jesus means demonstrating compassion. How can you make compassion a bigger part of your life and heart?

T—MATTHEW 16:6: "WATCH OUT AND BEWARE OF THE LEAVEN OF THE PHARISEES."

(See also Matthew 23:1–39, Mark 8:15, Mark 12:38, Luke 11:39–52, Luke 12:1, Luke 14:1, and Luke 20:46–47; seven references.)

Even if the religious leaders of Jesus's day had done everything they could to help the people instead of preying on them, it still would not have been enough. The world still needed a Savior. But Jesus is pointing out that the religious leaders could have at least helped Him in the process. Instead, they made it harder for Him to help people. In fact, it did not take long before they purposed in their hearts to kill Jesus. Quakers they were not!

Hate is ugly and can make a sane person do insane things. Hate can turn something beautiful into something ugly really fast. When hatred takes root, all perspective is lost, and it is difficult to get it back.

Jesus is telling us to stay as far away as possible from religious people who hate. Their fault was their hatred. They were not faulted for keeping the Law—Jesus Himself embraced the Law. They were faulted for hating. This is not talked about much in Christian circles. Religion is not bad. Religious leaders are not bad if they point to Jesus. But for some reason, within the human spirit there is a need to compete with Jesus. This was the downfall of the religious leaders of Jesus's day: they competed with Jesus. When they realized they were no match for Him, they did the only thing left, which was to plot to kill Him.

Had the religious leaders done what Jesus is asking us to do, the outcome could have been much different. Jesus came to redeem the religious leaders. This is the problem with being a religious leader: we think we can do it as well as Jesus, and we get jealous. The whole point of Jesus coming was not to compete with Him but to follow Him!

Gospel Grit Challenge: Is there any residue of hate in your heart? Ask God to help you if there is. If there is not, pray for someone you may know who is struggling with hate.

T—MATTHEW 16:15: "BUT WHO DO YOU SAY THAT I AM?"

One of the university courses I taught recently was philosophy. One of the common questions asked is this: "Does life have meaning and purpose?" We know that outside of Jesus Christ, life may not have either. But with Jesus Christ, life always has meaning and purpose. (Maybe someone should write a book on purpose; it might sell a few copies!)

Philosophy asks some interesting questions. However, the question asked by Jesus—"Who do you say I am?"—outweighs all the questions of philosophy put together. When we resolve this question with the proper response, then all the puzzle pieces begin to fall into place.

I absolutely dislike putting together puzzles, while my wife absolutely loves it. I bet I have not put together more than five puzzle pieces in thirty-one years of marriage. The Gospels are a little bit like a puzzle. I am hoping that by seeing the big picture in this book, the role of Jesus in your life will become more clear to you as you continue following Him. I am hoping you will examine your backpack and what's in it in light of following Jesus.

Jesus asks this question of each of us. We *must* solve it in our hearts. When we can settle the issue that Jesus is God, then all of life becomes smoother and begins to make a lot of sense.

Gospel Grit Challenge: Who is Jesus in your life? What if He were King of Kings and Lord of Lords in your life? How would you approach life then?
(See also Mark 11:22, Luke 5:20, Luke 7:9, Luke 17:6, and Luke 24:38; six references.)

> T—MATTHEW 17:20: "IF YOU HAVE FAITH THE SIZE OF A MUSTARD
> SEED, YOU WILL SAY TO THIS MOUNTAIN, 'MOVE FROM HERE TO THERE,'
> AND IT WILL MOVE; AND NOTHING WILL BE IMPOSSIBLE TO YOU."

Often in this study, a verse could go into a second or third category. There are far more references to faith than what I have categorized above, but these five are powerful references to the subject.

Jesus spent far more time demonstrating faith than He did teaching on faith. The calling of His disciples was a call to faith. The message He left His disciples was a call to faith. Jesus's dying, trusting He would rise from the dead, was faith in action. Jesus showed even greater faith in entrusting everything He stood for to His disciples before leaving them. The Gospels could easily be called the Gospels of Faith.

Faith is both easy and hard. If you are a child, you simply trust no matter what. That's faith. As adults we have a greater knowledge of life, so faith can be difficult for us. Yet, Jesus calls all to a life of faith and tells us to have faith like children.

Faith is hard when things do not work out. When things *do* work out, faith is easy—until the next time something comes along that requires it. I love the image of faith portrayed by Indiana Jones when he takes a step of faith seemingly into the abyss, only to have his foot land on a rock bridge—not because it was seen, but because it was unseen. After the first step, what was unseen becomes seen. It sounds easy, but in some circumstances walking in faith is very difficult to pull off.

A major element of following Jesus is trusting Him for what He does *not* say. We will not always have answers. That is what makes following Him so important. The closer we are to Him, the greater our faith becomes. If we follow Him at a distance, our faith weakens because we begin to look around at all the ways things can go wrong. Following closely allows us to see all that can go right. Faith is both that fragile and that powerful at the same time. I know this: He has never failed me. So I put my faith in Him. That is what it means to be a follower of Jesus

Christ. Following Jesus means looking at His backpack and what He can offer you, not yours and what you can do for yourself.

Gospel Grit Challenge: Where do you need to have a greater faith? Has God ever let you down? Can you think of anyone better to put your faith in than Jesus Christ? You can trust Him.
(See also Matthew 18:4, Matthew 18:5, Matthew 18:6, Matthew 18:10, Mark 9:36, Mark 9:37, Mark 10:13–14, Mark 10:15, Mark 10:16, Luke 9:48, and Luke 18:16–17; twelve references.)

I love the frequency with which Jesus references children in the

---

T—MATTHEW 18:3: "UNLESS YOU ARE CONVERTED AND BECOME LIKE CHILDREN, YOU WILL NOT ENTER THE KINGDOM OF HEAVEN."

Gospels. Remember, He is wandering the streets and the countryside, and He is bound to run into children. Further, an important part of Jesus's teaching included children. In fact, on the most important issue of His teaching, which is salvation, He tells all of us that we are to come to Him as children.

Several years ago I began our church year with a passage of Scripture in Isaiah that spoke about becoming an oak of righteousness. From that day forward we began calling our children acorns, and it is our desire for our children to become oaks of righteousness. I gave our congregation twenty-one things I would love for our children by age twenty-one. They are:

1. To love God with all their heart, mind, soul, and strength.
2. To love all people groups.
3. To love the Word of God.
4. To love the church.
5. To love Christian service.
6. To love worshiping God with one's entire being.
7. To seek a calling of ministry from God.
8. To love and obey parents.

9. To have integrity/honesty.
10. To focus on studies and spiritual development.
11. To practice Philippians 4:8 pertaining to all forms of entertainment.
12. To develop a good work ethic.
13. To have high moral standards.
14. To have a strong belief in a literal heaven and a literal hell.
15. To support missionaries and mission work for God.
16. To be soul winners.
17. To be filled with the Holy Spirit.
18. To prize Christian unity.
19. To be a generous giver.
20. To help the poor.
21. To be a follower of Jesus Christ.

Children are important to Jesus. Children should be our highest priority in the church. Children must be where we put our efforts in order to have a better tomorrow.

Gospel Grit Challenge: No matter how old you are, which of the above twenty-one areas need strengthening in your life?

T—MATTHEW 18:15: "IF YOUR BROTHER SINS, GO SHOW HIM HIS FAULT IN PRIVATE."

This is one of the hardest teachings in the Gospels to follow. It is difficult because it requires confrontation, and most of us do not like confrontation. We avoid it at all costs. I didn't mind it when I was younger, but the older I get the less I like confronting people.

Thankfully, Jesus instructs us to go to our brother in private. The reference to a "brother" infers we are both followers of Jesus Christ. The obvious reason to go in private is so there will be less bloodshed (figuratively speaking!) and fewer people will know about the situation. People like a bloody story. Jesus is trying to help us avoid bloodshed.

This goes beyond just patching up a fight. Jesus is teaching us to make the fault of another a moment for transformation. Jesus wants this to be a moment when followers of His learn to work things out because of Him. When He said this, only Jesus knew He would not be sticking around. The disciples had not even an inclination at this point that Jesus would be leaving them for good in a short while. They thought this party was only going to get bigger, better, and brighter. They didn't know they would have to learn to stand by one another through some very difficult times and remain united in the face of a lot of opposition.

I have confronted numerous people using this teaching. Once in a while it doesn't turn out well. Most of the time, the confrontation turns out great. The outcome is not our problem so much as being obedient to this teaching. The problem with avoidance is that we are burying something alive, and it usually comes back twice as bad the next time around!

Gospel Grit Challenge: Is there anybody in your life you need to confront to make things better for all? Remember a previous teaching Jesus gave us on first taking the beam out of our own eye. Allow God to search your own life first.

T—MATTHEW 18:16: "BUT IF HE DOES NOT LISTEN TO YOU, TAKE ONE OR TWO MORE WITH YOU, SO THAT BY THE MOUTH OF TWO OR THREE WITNESSES EVERY FACT MAY BE CONFIRMED."

This is the sequel to the previous verse. In cases of conflict, we are to first go to a person in private. If that does not work, then this verse addresses what is to come next. The goal is not to hang the person; the goal is to resolve the problem.

For me, the most important phrase in this teaching is "every fact." It is important because this is what we do the worst job of in Christianity. We are guilty of condemning people without getting all the facts. We are notorious for making judgments based on what one person has to say and not really being interested in what all the parties have to say. This is wrong. This is deadly. This is poison.

Jesus is giving us a marvelous opportunity to make crooked lines straight using this method of confrontation. Amazingly, this is what is done in police work. The job of a detective is to discover every fact in a case. Until every fact is uncovered, judgments are to be withheld. It is fair to have suspicions, but detectives are to make no premature judgments because that can change the outcome.

As a chaplain for a local police department, I experience some interesting situations. One day while at the department, a murder suspect was brought in. I was not there to see the suspect, only to bring support to the police involved in the case and to the victim's family. Surprisingly, the suspect asked for a chaplain. I was neither a priest nor in a position to visit with this man. But the detective asked if I would sit with him and listen and visit while I would be watched and recorded.

I did not have the power or the authority to set this man free. Nor did I want to do so. Jesus is teaching us in this passage that we have both the power and the authority to help set people free by gathering the facts, helping people see the error of their ways, and giving them second chances. After all, isn't that what following Jesus is all about? He is a God who is forever giving us yet another chance to follow Him more closely!

Gospel Grit Challenge: When you have judged people, did you get all the facts from both sides of the aisle? Is there a chance you could be wrong about someone?

T—MATTHEW 18:18: "WHATEVER YOU WILL BIND ON EARTH SHALL BE BOUND IN HEAVEN; AND WHATEVER YOU LOOSE ON EARTH SHALL BE LOOSED IN HEAVEN."

This is the conclusion of the previous two teachings from Jesus. Jesus is telling us that there are eternal implications to how we handle relationships on earth. He is telling us that what is done on earth will have strong connections to what takes place in heaven.

For reasons explained in the afterword, I deliberately left out the passages on heaven and hell that are part of Jesus's teachings. However, this passage references heaven and the impact we can have in heaven while living on earth. The subject is not so much about the afterlife as it is taking care of business properly right now.

It is daunting to think that what we do today can have an impact ten thousand years from now. Most of the time, I am sure we do not think in these terms. Jesus is telling us that we should. Everything He did had an eternal purpose to it. Everything we do ought to have an eternal purpose as well.

The context of this verse is correcting one another. We are to help one another be successful. Admittedly, there are some people we may not want to help. Following Jesus demands we move beyond prejudice and bias and be Jesus to people who need Him the most.

Gospel Grit Challenge: Is there any relationship in your life that needs cleaning up? Is there anyone whom you need to forgive today?

T—MATTHEW 20:16: "THE LAST SHALL BE FIRST, AND THE FIRST LAST."

(See also Matthew 20:26, Matthew 20:27, Mark 9:35, Mark 10:31, Luke 6:36, Luke 8:21, Luke 9:26, Luke 11:28, Luke 11:41, Luke 22:26, John 3:21, John 13:8, and John 13:15; fourteen references.)

The entire reason Jesus came to earth was to serve a fallen race: us! Jesus came to serve us because in serving ourselves we destroy ourselves. All roots of sin come through self-serving. Jesus came to turn the models of the world upside down. Jesus came to show the world that if God Himself served the poorest of the poor, then we should follow His example and serve all mankind.

Kings are supposed to be served. Presidents are likewise served. They do not serve the common people. They say they do, but they really don't. In the United States of America, presidents are famous and rich when they leave office. One president in recent memory I can commend at this point is Jimmy Carter and his Habitat for Humanity projects. He is not sitting in a plush office running his postpresidency. Jimmy Carter is pounding nails and cutting boards. For this, I commend him. He possibly has done far more good for the world after his presidency than when he was president!

The Bible declares Jesus is the King of Kings and the Lord of Lords. Of all people who should be served, He is foremost. Yet, He told us that He came to serve. That is what He showed us too!

Being a follower of Jesus Christ is *all* about serving other people. If we are not serving someone else, we are serving ourselves. Jesus gave us a cure to enhance our lives by serving others. His plan is simply genius. Would we not admit that after serving someone, we feel great inside? It is far more satisfying helping someone else than serving our own selfish needs. Yet we struggle with prioritizing others over ourselves. If we can determine to stay close to Jesus, we will find ourselves helping others more than we find ourselves serving our own selfish interests.

One of the things I try to do every day is to help at least one person in a definitive way. It does not have to cost anything or take a huge amount of time. I just want to help at least one person a day in some way. At the end of the year, I can measure this one area of my life by knowing I helped 365 or more people in a year! Try it, you might like it!

Self-serving also tends to be linked to materialistic living. The more toys we have, the more likely we are to serve ourselves. Take a look in your backpack and see how many toys you have in there. Perhaps today would be a good day to have a garage sale. Take a look in Jesus's backpack; you won't find very many toys!

Gospel Grit Challenge: Where are you currently serving Jesus? Whom are you serving?

T—MATTHEW 22:37: "YOU SHALL LOVE THE LORD YOUR GOD WITH ALL YOUR HEART, AND WITH ALL YOUR SOUL, AND WITH ALL YOUR MIND."

(See also Matthew 22:39, John 13:1, John 13:34–35, John 14:21, John 14:23, John 15:9, John 15:10, John 15:12, and John 15:17; ten references.)

God is love. Jesus is love. The Gospels are love. The Bible is love. Everything Jesus stands for is all about love. Love is what pushed Him out of heaven. Love is what gave Him a reason to get up in the morning after coming to earth (and some days probably wondering what in the world He was doing here!).

Following Jesus means to embrace love. When we embrace love, we embrace people. Love is the cure to just about every messed-up relationship in the world. Trust and forgiveness are subsets of love. Love is at the heart of following Jesus because it is at the heart of Jesus!

I don't want to make these teachings a commentary, so I have avoided breaking each verse down. I have tried to stay general, with broad, sweeping themes, stories, illustrations, and anecdotes. This teaching, however, demands more. It is a teaching that encompasses our entire being. It teaches us that following Jesus is all-consuming and should consume all of us.

Jesus breaks love down into three categories to include heart, soul, and mind. He leaves no stone unturned. He makes sure that when we exercise love, we exercise our entire being. This is the essence of following Jesus: to involve our entire being. Love is not a switch or a faucet we turn on and off. Love is a rushing river that flows freely, splashing those who get close enough to feel its effects.

Gospel Grit Challenge: Heart, soul, mind: which one needs development in your life? Begin with where you see love in action in your life and then where you see love withheld. These are your starting points.

T—MATTHEW 24:4: "SEE TO IT THAT NO ONE MISLEADS YOU."

I have addressed this warning in other verses, but I choose to address it yet again. I believe Jesus puts such a heavy emphasis on this theme because He knows we are easily led astray. Our biblical worldview may not be as biblical as we would like to think.

The harsh reality is that many Christians cannot defend their faith or their beliefs with Scripture. We guess and we make things up, hoping we are close. The starting point for being misled is to be ignorant of what the Bible says. Another starting point is not following Jesus closely enough in relationship, leaving us open to being led astray by another voice. It happens all the time. I have seen it too many times to count.

The greatest culprits in this scheme are fellow Christians who want someone to support their beliefs, so they convince others with their influence and their false godliness that a given thing is what Jesus would do or teach when in reality they haven't one single Scripture to back them up.

As Christians, we need to stop guessing at our beliefs and stop guessing at what Jesus has showed us and told us. When we are closely following Jesus, we are less likely to be led astray. It really is that simple!

Gospel Grit Challenge: Are you willing to write down Scriptures that support your core values? Put another way, are you willing to adjust your core values if they do not line up with Scripture?

T—MATTHEW 24:33: "RECOGNIZE THAT HE IS NEAR, RIGHT AT THE DOOR."

I use this verse to remind us of an important "following Jesus" principle: Jesus is close by. He never is far away. When we follow Him, He does not run ahead of us, trying to ditch us for a better date.

Not only is Jesus near, but in the context of this teaching, so is His return. This is very exciting to think about. I know people who do not like to think about the return of Jesus. It is as though they have something better planned for the week. Are you kidding me? There is nothing better than being with Jesus in heaven forever and ever.

Having a child is awesome. Having a great career is rewarding. Having a lucrative retirement is reassuring. Having a clean bill of health is a huge relief. Looking forward to an extended vacation is nothing but pleasure. You can assemble all the wonderful things there are in this life, but together they will fall far short of being with Jesus. That is why following Him now is a great way to live, because the better we get to know Him today, the better the relationship will be tomorrow and on into eternity. This is the essence of following Jesus.

Gospel Grit Challenge: Is your house in order for the return of Jesus for you? What more do you need to accomplish before Jesus comes for you? Get 'er done!

T—MATTHEW 25:35–46: "FOR I WAS HUNGRY, AND YOU GAVE ME SOMETHING TO EAT; I WAS THIRSTY, AND YOU GAVE ME SOMETHING TO DRINK; I WAS A STRANGER, AND YOU INVITED ME IN; NAKED, AND YOU CLOTHED ME; I WAS SICK, AND YOU VISITED ME; I WAS IN PRISON, AND YOU CAME TO ME."

Many think this teaching is a great job description for followers of Jesus Christ, and they're almost right. Actually, it is one half of the job description. The other half is leading people to a saving knowledge of Jesus Christ. If you put this verse together with all the verses that deal with salvation, you have a nutshell look at what Jesus was showing us and telling us in order to be His followers.

Jesus is telling us that when we do something for someone less fortunate, we have done it for or to Him. We are doing the act of love as though Jesus Himself were the recipient. This verse is the flesh on Luke 4:18–19: "The Spirit of the Lord is upon Me, because He has anointed Me to preach the gospel to the poor. He has sent me to proclaim release to the captives, and recovery of sight to the blind, to set free those who are downtrodden. To proclaim the favorable year of the Lord."

I visited people in Haiti who were naked. I have been to the hospital to visit people who were sick. I have given food to the hungry. I have visited inmates in prison. I have done each of these ticket items from this teaching, but rarely do I think I am doing it to Jesus. I look at people for what they are: people like you and me who have been on a bit of a different journey. Jesus wants us to know they are important. This is what He is teaching.

Jesus is always teaching the value of life. Jesus, the giver of eternal life, is definitely pro-life. He came to conquer death. How could He be anything else but pro-life! Nowhere in the Gospels does Jesus end a life. Even in His death, He gave life to us.

Gospel Grit Challenge: Who do you need to help today? Look for the face of Jesus through a person who is hungry, thirsty, naked, a stranger, or in trouble with the law. Wait a minute…that was Jesus too!

S—MATTHEW 26:26–30: "JESUS SANG A HYMN WITH HIS DISCIPLES."

Don't you just love the way Scripture is used for personal gain or to prove a point? Actually, I am being totally sarcastic. Some would use this as a proof text for using only hymns in church. Not the point at all! The point is that Jesus incorporated music into His life. Wouldn't you love to know the tune He was singing? Wouldn't you love to know the words to the tune? Wouldn't you love to know what kind of a voice Jesus had?

Music is a part of following Jesus, and it touches the soul like nothing else can. It is uplifting to our hearts and lives.

I have never had a good voice, but I had to lead music in our church in the early years because there was nobody else to do it. I remember when we had a children's musical. "Psalty" musicals were really popular at the time—led by a cartoony character who is a big, blue psalter or hymnbook. You guessed it; I was Psalty. I got all dressed up in that big blue box with that blue makeup and tight blue nylons and played the part. When it came time for the solo, I would turn my back to the audience, kneel down as though I was being superspiritual, and move my arms a bunch, and out would come this beautiful solo from behind the platform. It was the director's husband, who has a beautiful George Beverly Shea voice. People were stunned at how well I was singing until I am sure most figured out who it really was.

Out of the twelve disciples, I am sure there were a few clunkers in the group like me. The point is not how well we sing, but that we sing! If singing wasn't a part of following Jesus, this verse would not have made the final cut in the Gospels.

Gospel Grit Challenge: When you go to church do you sing or stare and listen? No matter what you sound like, follow Jesus and sing!

T—MATTHEW 26:37: "JESUS BEGAN TO BE GRIEVED AND DISTRESSED."

This statement is significant because it shows us several things on several levels. One, we see the humanity of Jesus. Two, the verse shows us how serious the upcoming events were in His mind. Three, we see that even in the life of Jesus, there were going to be some less-than-happy days. Part of following Jesus is realizing there are going to be some great days, some gray days, and some dark days. They are all a part of following Him.

Imagine having the power to know, as Jesus did, what your fate would soon be. More than that, imagine having the power to stop it but so much love that you wouldn't dare. Imagine being totally and completely innocent and knowing you would be treated worse than a prisoner who was guilty beyond a reasonable doubt. Imagine having the ability to call down fire from heaven, yet settling for vinegar to quench your thirst. Imagine having the power to send every Roman soldier and every angry Jew to hell for what they were about to do to you, yet dying for them instead!

When we give it careful thought and study, we recognize that the cross is the single most amazing event in human history. It is not as though Jesus did not know what was coming. Before the creation of the world, He knew exactly what His fate would be. He had an eternity to discuss it with the Father, yet They chose as their plan the cross.

I had my first major surgery a few years ago. As soon as the doctor told me the date, I centered my life on that day. Everything I did up to the surgery had everything to do *with* the surgery, including what I ate, how I slept, and how I cared for my body. Everything Jesus did up to the point of dying on the cross had everything to do with dying on the cross. It was His central focus, and He did not waver from it.

Gospel Grit Challenge: What has caused grieving and distress in your life? Be glad Jesus has walked that road before you and you can share those thoughts with Him. He would love to hear from you!

T—MATTHEW 26:38: "KEEP WATCH WITH ME."

This teaching is huge. It tells us we are in this thing together with Jesus. We may be following Him, but we are together in the arena of life. Jesus never taught that it was all about Him and the rest of us poor saps would be lucky if we even got to spend a few brief moments with Him. No, He invites us to carry the cross and join Him. Did I tell you that eventually Jesus trades His backpack in for a cross? To many, that does not sound like a good deal. I will have much more to say about that trade-in in the next passage.

One afternoon I was hunting in the mountains of eastern Oregon. I remember the dense forest and the steep terrain. I remember resting my weary body, setting down my gun, and taking a nap! I was awakened by an eerie feeling that something was watching me. My premonition was right. As I turned around ever so slowly, at the end of what I would esti-mate to be a fifty-foot log was the most beautiful white timber wolf I had ever seen. I had just read in a hunting magazine the week before about this beautiful creature and their ability to hunt. Yikes! I had also read they were endangered.

I slowly got to my feet, grabbing my rifle all in one motion. With my sights on that wolf, we stood opposed to one another, staking out our territory on each end of the log. The wolf was a good fifteen feet above me, stooped down in a crouch with his teeth showing. Seriously, I am not making this up! We stared one another down, and after what seemed to be hours (but I am sure was only minutes), he turned and ran up and over the hill and out of sight.

Had I kept better watch, I would never have found myself in that position. I did not know there were wolves in the area. I figured I was safe. This is much like life. We figure we are safe. We figure the wolves are somewhere else, bothering people in some other part of the world. Wrong! They stand at our front door waiting for us to let down our guard. Jesus tells us to keep watch with Him. As a follower of Jesus, it is our responsibility to keep watch!

Gospel Grit Challenge: In what ways have you let down your guard? What steps can you take to become alert again as a follower of Jesus Christ?

T—MATTHEW 26:52: "PUT YOUR SWORD BACK INTO ITS PLACE; FOR ALL THOSE WHO TAKE UP THE SWORD SHALL PERISH BY THE SWORD."

(See also Matthew 26:63, Matthew 26:67, Matthew 27:11, Matthew 27:12, Matthew 27:14, Matthew 27:46, Mark 10:45, Mark 14:61, Mark 15:5, Luke 23:9, Luke 23:34, Luke 23:46, Luke 24:40, John 17:1, John 16:33, John 17:1, John 18:4, John 18:11, and John 19:1; twenty references.)

For Jesus, this is the conclusion to the journey on earth. He came that He might die on the cross. What began with a backpack, a few disciples, no place to lay His head, no post office box number, no place to shower, and no place to shop for clothes ended on Calvary. Jesus came to this earth to die for my sins and yours.

The day came when Jesus had walked this earth in ministry for three years. At the conclusion of those three years, He had collected in His backpack all of the sin, all of the sickness, all that is wrong in this world. Then Jesus traded in His backpack for a cross. Some would say that was a bad deal for Jesus. Actually, it was the only way to rid Him of the burdens He had collected. He shifted them over to the cross and killed them. It was the only way to rid Himself of His burden and ours!

I have been known to make some really bad car deals in my life. If there is a lemon on the lot, I will find it, buy it, and make the car dealer laugh all the way to the bank! But Jesus knew what He was doing. Jesus did not deserve the cross. The cross was necessary! The cross is necessary today!

It has become popular to remove the cross from public property and government buildings. There are even some churches that are removing crosses from their churches because the cross is offensive. We built our newer sanctuary about ten years ago. After building it, the architect realized that if the cross was to go up front, it would be in the way of the two jumbo screens on the wall. I told the committee that was perfect. It was perfect because the cross was *meant* to be in the way. The cross was not meant to be placed in a corner where nobody could see it. The cross was meant to be the center of Christianity! So we have three crosses in the front of our sanctuary, all life-size: one on each landing for the two thieves who made their eternal life choices, and one in the center that gets in the way of every song we sing and every announcement we make and every video we show.

If we are going to follow Jesus, there will come a day when He asks us to trade in our backpack for a cross. It is then we are truly followers of Jesus Christ!

Gospel Grit Challenge: How close are you to turning in your backpack? Can you trust that God will give you something better than you can fit in that old backpack?

S—MATTHEW 28:3: "HIS APPEARANCE WAS LIKE LIGHTNING, AND HIS GARMENT AS WHITE AS SNOW."

The bottom line for followers of Jesus is not this life, but the life that is to come. The resurrection is the final act in this play we call life. For the follower of Christ, it is the beginning of eternal life in heaven with Jesus and all who have gone before us.

After the homegoing of my sixteen-year-old son, Kevin, all I really wanted was to be in heaven. Half of me was here, but the other half of my heart was in heaven. After ten years, that has not changed—except that now I am ten years closer to seeing him!

For the longest time after the Lord called my son to heaven, I longed for the day when I would see Kevin again. I miss him more than words can tell. Please listen to what I am about to write. As time passed, my desire to see Kevin did not necessarily diminish, but my desire to see someone else grew stronger until the day I realized my desire to see this someone else had surpassed my desire to see my son.

That someone else is Jesus Christ. He is the one who died for me and made eternal life possible. He is the one who is going to make the reunion with my loved ones possible forever and ever, never to be separated again. Jesus is the one who is offering me a home where there is no more sorrow, suffering, pain, mourning, tears, or death. I could go on and on, but this is not a study on heaven. However, the one I want to see and thank and praise and love for the first thousand years is Jesus Christ. You bet I am going to follow Him wherever He leads me. I challenge you to do the same!

Gospel Grit Challenge: Whatever you are looking forward to most in this life, it pales in comparison to meeting the one whom you are following: Jesus Christ. Following Christ is worth it. Never give up following Jesus!

SCRIPTURES FROM MATTHEW FOR FURTHER STUDY

In the list below, the Scriptures are numbered. They include all Scriptures discussed in the chapter as well as those referenced in Matthew. As in the chapter discussions, "T" denotes "told"; "S" denotes "showed." I strongly encourage you to sit down with this list, your Bible, and a notebook, and go on a journey of your own through this amazing gospel!

1. T—Matthew 3:15: "Fulfill all righteousness."
2. S—Matthew 3:15: Jesus was baptized.
3. S—Matthew 3:16: The Spirit of God descended on Jesus.
4. S—Matthew 3:17: "This is My Son with whom I am pleased."
5. S—Matthew 4:1: Jesus was led by the Spirit into the wilderness to be tempted by the devil.
6. S—Matthew 4:2: He fasted forty days and forty nights and became hungry.
7. T—Matthew 4:4: "It is written, 'Man shall not live on bread alone, but on every word that proceeds out of the mouth of God.'"
8. T—Matthew 4:7: "It is written, 'You shall not put the Lord your God to the test.'"
9. T—Matthew 4:10: "Go Satan! For it is written, 'You shall worship the Lord your God, and serve Him only."
10. T—Matthew 4:17: Jesus began to preach and say, "Repent, for the kingdom of heaven is at hand."
11 T—Matthew 4:19: "Follow Me, and I will make you fishers of men."
12. S—Matthew 4:23: Jesus taught in the synagogues, proclaiming the gospel of the kingdom and healing diseases and sickness.
13. T—Matthew 5:3: "Blessed are the poor in spirit."
14. T—Matthew 5:4: "Blessed are those who mourn."
15. T—Matthew 5:5: "Blessed are the gentle."

16. T—Matthew 5:6: "Blessed are those who hunger and thirst for righteousness."

17. T—Matthew 5:7: "Blessed are the merciful."

18. T—Matthew 5:8: "Blessed are the pure in heart."

19. T—Matthew 5:9: "Blessed are the peacemakers."

20. T—Matthew 5:10: "Blessed are those who have been persecuted for the sake of righteousness."

21. T—Matthew 5:11: "Blessed are you when people insult you and persecute you, and falsely say all kinds of evil against you."

22. T—Matthew 5:12: "Rejoice and be glad."

23. T—Matthew 5:13: "You are the salt of the earth."

24. T—Matthew 5:14: "You are the light of the world."

25. T—Matthew 5:16: "Let your light shine before men in such a way that they may see your good deeds."

26. T—Matthew 5:17: "Do not think that I came to abolish the Law or the Prophets; I did not come to abolish but to fulfill."

27. T—Matthew 5:19: "Whoever then annuls one of the least of these commandments, and teaches others to do the same, shall be called least in the kingdom of heaven; but whoever keeps and teaches them, he shall be called great in the kingdom of heaven."

28. T—Matthew 5:20: "Unless your righteousness surpasses that of the scribes and Pharisees, you will not enter the kingdom of heaven."

29. T—Matthew 5:22: "Everyone who is angry with his brother shall be guilty before the court; and whoever says, 'You fool,' shall be guilty enough to go into the fiery hell."

30. T—Matthew 5:24: "First be reconciled to your brother, and then come and present your offering."

31. T—Matthew 5:25: "Make friends quickly with your opponent at law."

32. T—Matthew 5:28: "Everyone who looks at a woman with lust for her has already committed adultery with her in his heart."

33. T—Matthew 5:29: "If your right eye makes you stumble, tear it out."

34. T—Matthew 5:30: "If your right hand makes you stumble, cut it off."

35. T—Matthew 5:32: "Everyone who divorces his wife, except for the cause of unchastity, makes her commit adultery; and whoever marries a divorced woman commits adultery."

36. T—Matthew 5:34: "Make no oath at all."

37. T—Matthew 5:37: "Let your statement be, 'Yes, yes' or 'No, no.'"

38. T—Matthew 5:39: "Do not resist an evil person; but whoever slaps you on your right cheek, turn the other to him also."

39. T—Matthew 5:40: "If anyone wants to sue you, and take your shirt, let him have your coat also."

40. T—Matthew 5:42: "Give to him who asks of you, and do not turn away from him who wants to borrow from you."

41. T—Matthew 5:44: "Love your enemies and pray for those who persecute you."

42. T—Matthew 5:48: "Therefore, you are to be perfect, as your heavenly Father is perfect."

43. T—Matthew 6:1: "Beware of practicing your righteousness before men to be noticed by them."

44. T—Matthew 6:3: "When you give to the poor, do not let your left hand know what your right hand is doing."

45. T—Matthew 6:6: "When you pray, go into your inner room, close your door and pray to your Father who is in secret."

46. T—Matthew 6:7: "When you are praying, do not use meaningless repetition."

47. T—Matthew 6:9–13: "Pray, then, in this way: Our Father who is in heaven, hallowed be Your name. Your kingdom come. Your will be done, on earth as it is in heaven. Give us this day our daily bread. And forgive us our debts, as we also have forgiven our debtors. And do not lead us into temptation, but deliver us from evil."

48. T—Matthew 6:14: "If you forgive others...your heavenly Father will also forgive you."

49. T—Matthew 6:15: "If you do not forgive others, then your Father

will not forgive your transgressions."

50 T—Matthew 6:17: "When you fast, anoint your head and wash your face."

51. T—Matthew 6:19: "Do not store up for yourselves treasures on earth."

52. T—Matthew 6:20: "Store up for yourselves treasures in heaven."

53. T—Matthew 6:24: "No one can serve two masters; you cannot serve God and wealth."

54. T—Matthew 6:25: "Do not worry about your life, as to what you shall eat, or what you shall drink; nor for your body, as to what you shall put on."

55. T—Matthew 6:33: "Seek first His kingdom and His righteousness."

56. T—Matthew 6:34: "Do not worry about tomorrow."

57. T—Matthew 7:1: "Do not judge."

58. T—Matthew 7:5: "First take the log out of your own eye."

59. T—Matthew 7:6: "Do not give what is holy to dogs, and do not throw your pearls before swine."

60. T—Matthew 7:7: "Ask, and it will be given to you; seek, and you will find; knock, and it will be opened to you."

61. T—Matthew 7:12: "Treat people the same way you want them to treat you."

62. T—Matthew 7:13: "Enter through the narrow gate."

63. T—Matthew 7:15: "Beware of the false prophets."

64. T—Matthew 7:21: "Not everyone who says to Me, 'Lord, Lord,' will enter the kingdom of heaven, but he who does the will of My Father who is in heaven will enter."

65. T—Matthew 7:24: "Everyone who hears these words of Mine and acts on them, may be compared to a wise man."

66. T—Matthew 7:26: "Everyone who hears these words of Mine and does not act on them, will be like a foolish man."

67. S—Matthew 7:29: "He taught them as one having authority."

68. S—Matthew 8:3: He stretched out His hand and touched the leper.

69. S—Matthew 8:13: He healed the paralyzed servant of the centurion.

70. S—Matthew 8:15: He healed Peter's mother-in-law.
71. S—Matthew 8:16: He cast out demons and healed all who were sick.
72. S—Matthew 8:18: He saw the crowd and gave orders to depart to the other side.
73. T—Matthew 8:22: "Follow Me, and allow the dead to bury their own dead."
74. S—Matthew 8:24: He was asleep in the boat in a storm.
75. S—Matthew 8:26: He rebuked the wind and it became perfectly calm.
76. S—Matthew 8:32: He cast out demons from two men into some pigs.
77. S—Matthew 8:34: Jesus was asked to leave.
78. S—Matthew 9:2: He forgave sin.
79. S—Matthew 9:6: He healed the paralytic.
80. T—Matthew 9:9: He said, "Follow Me" to Matthew.
81. S—Matthew 9:10: Jesus dined with many sinners.
82. T—Matthew 9:13: "Go and learn what this means."
83. S—Matthew 9:22: Jesus healed a woman who believed all she had to do was touch Him for healing.
84. S—Matthew 9:25: Jesus brought a dead girl back to life.
85. S—Matthew 9:29–30: Jesus healed two blind men.
86. S—Matthew 9:33: Jesus cast a demon out of a mute man.
87. S—Matthew 9:35: Jesus went to the cities and villages teaching in their synagogues, proclaiming the gospel of the kingdom, and healing every kind of disease and sickness.
88. S—Matthew 9:36: Seeing the multitudes, He felt compassion.
89. T—Matthew 9:38: "Beseech the Lord of the harvest to send out workers into His harvest."
90. S—Matthew 10:1: He summoned His twelve disciples and gave them authority to cast out unclean spirits and to heal every kind of disease and every kind of sickness.
91. S—Matthew 10:5: Jesus sent out those twelve after instructing them.

92. T—Matthew 10:5–6: "Do not go to…the Gentiles…but rather go to the lost sheep of the house of Israel."

93. T—Matthew 10:7: "Preach, saying, 'The kingdom of heaven is at hand.'"

94. T—Matthew 10:8: "Heal the sick, raise the dead, cleanse the lepers, cast out demons."

95. T—Matthew 10:9: "Do not acquire gold, or silver, or copper for your money belts."

96. S—Matthew 10:11: He told the twelve that when they arrived at a city, they were to inquire who was worthy in the city and stay there.

97. T—Matthew 10:12: "As you enter the house, give it your greeting."

98. T—Matthew 10:14: "Whoever does not receive you…shake the dust off your feet."

99. T—Matthew 10:16: "Be shrewd as serpents and innocent as doves."

100. T—Matthew 10:17: "But beware of men."

101. T—Matthew 10:19: "Do not worry about how or what you are to say."

102. T—Matthew 10:20: "It is not you who speak, but it is the Spirit of your Father who speaks in you."

103. T—Matthew 10:22: "It is the one who has endured to the end who will be saved."

104. T—Matthew 10:23: "Whenever they persecute you in one city, flee to the next."

105. T—Matthew 10:26: "Do not fear them."

106. T—Matthew 10:27: "What I tell you in the darkness, speak in the light; and what you hear whispered in your ear, proclaim among the housetops."

107. T—Matthew 10:28: "Do not fear those who kill the body."

108. T—Matthew 10:31: "Do not fear."

109. T—Matthew 10:32: "Everyone who confesses Me before men, I will also confess him before My father who is in heaven."

110. T—Matthew 10:33: "Whoever denies Me before men, I will also deny him before My Father who is in heaven."

111. T—Matthew 10:34: "I did not come to bring peace, but a sword."

112. T—Matthew 10:37: "He who loves father or mother…and…son or daughter more than Me is not worthy of Me."

113. T—Matthew 10:38: "And he who does not take his cross and follow after Me is not worthy of Me."

114. T—Matthew 10:39: "He who has found his life will lose it, and he who has lost his life for My sake will find it."

115. S—Matthew 11:1: He departed from there to teach and preach in their cities.

116. T—Matthew 11:5: "The blind receive sight and the lame walk, the lepers are cleansed and the deaf hear, the dead are raised up, and the poor have the gospel preached to them."

117. S—Matthew 11:20: He began to reproach the cities in which most of His miracles were done because they did not repent.

118. T—Matthew 11:25: "I praise You, Father."

119. T—Matthew 11:28–29: "Come to Me, all who are weary and heavy-laden, and I will give you rest. Take My yoke upon you and learn from Me, for I am gentle and humble in heart, and you will find rest for your souls."

120. S—Matthew 12:13: Jesus healed the man's hand on the Sabbath.

121. S—Matthew 12:15: He healed them all.

122. S—Matthew 12:22: Jesus healed, and He cast out a demon from a possessed man.

123. T—Matthew 12:30: "He who is not with Me is against Me; and he who does not gather with me scatters."

124. T—Matthew 12:31: "Whoever speaks against [blasphemes] the Holy Spirit, it shall not be forgiven him."

125. T—Matthew 12:37: "By your words you will be justified, and by your words you will be condemned."

126. T—Matthew 12:50: "Whoever does the will of My Father who is in heaven, he is My brother and sister and mother."

127. S—Matthew 13:3: He spoke many things to them in parables.

128. T—Matthew 13:12: "For whoever has, to him shall more be given, and he will have an abundance; but whoever does not have, even what he has shall be taken away from him."

129. T—Matthew 13:16: "Blessed are your eyes, because they see; and your ears, because they hear."

130. T—Matthew 13:18–23: Parable of the four kinds of seed.

131. T—Matthew 13:24–30: Parable of the tares and wheat.

132. T—Matthew 13:31–32: Parable of the mustard seed.

133. T—Matthew 13:33: Parable of the leaven.

134. T—Matthew 13:36–50: Explanation of the four parables.

135. S—Matthew 13:54: He began teaching in the synagogue.

136. T—Matthew 13:57: "A prophet is not without honor except in his hometown and in his own household."

137. S—Matthew 13:58: He did not do many miracles there because of their unbelief.

138. S—Matthew 14:13: When He heard about John the Baptist's death, He withdrew to a lonely place by Himself.

139. S—Matthew 14:14: He felt compassion and healed the sick.

140. S—Matthew 14:19: He blessed the food and gave it away.

141. S—Matthew 14:22: He sent the multitudes away.

142. S—Matthew 14:23: He went up to the mountain by Himself to pray; He was there alone.

143. S—Matthew 14:25: He came to them walking on the sea.

144. T—Matthew 14:27: "Take courage; it is I; do not be afraid."

145. S—Matthew 14:28: Peter asked Jesus to command him to come to Him on the water.

146. S—Matthew 14:31: Immediately, Jesus stretched out His hand and took hold of him.

147. S—Matthew 14:36: As many as touched the fringe of His cloak were healed.

148. T—Matthew 15:11: "It is not what enters into the mouth that defiles the man, but what proceeds out of the mouth, this defiles the man."

149. T—Matthew 15:24: "I was sent only to the lost sheep of the house of Israel."
150. S—Matthew 15:28: He healed a demon-possessed daughter.
151. S—Matthew 15:30: He healed them.
152. T—Matthew 15:32: "I feel compassion for the people."
153. S—Matthew 15:36: He took the seven loaves and the fish, gave thanks for them, broke them and started giving them to the disciples to give to the people.
154. S—Matthew 15:39: He sent away the crowds.
155. S—Matthew 16:4: He left them and went away.
156. T—Matthew 16:6: "Watch out and beware of the leaven of the Pharisees and Sadducees."
157. T—Matthew 16:15: "But who do you say that I am?"
158. S—Matthew 16:21: He said He must suffer, be killed, and be raised up on the third day.
159. T—Matthew 16:24: "If anyone wishes to come after Me, he must deny himself, and take up his cross and follow Me."
160. T—Matthew 17:7: "Get up, and do not be afraid."
161. S—Matthew 17:18: Jesus rebukes a demon in a boy, and the boy is healed.
162. T—Matthew 17:20: "If you have faith the size of a mustard seed, you will say to this mountain, 'Move from here to there,' and it will move; and nothing will be impossible to you."
163. T—Matthew 17:21: "This kind does not go out except for prayer and fasting."
164. —Matthew 17:24–25: Tax collectors inquired about whether or not Jesus paid a particular tax. The answer was yes.
165. T—Matthew 18:3: "Unless you are converted and become like children, you will not enter the kingdom of heaven."
166. T—Matthew 18:4: "Whoever then humbles himself as this child, he is the greatest in the kingdom of heaven."
167. T—Matthew 18:5: "Whoever receives one such child in My name receives Me."

168. T—Matthew 18:6: "Whoever causes one of these little ones who believe in Me to stumble, it would be better for him to have a heavy millstone hung around his neck, and to be drowned in the depth of the sea."

169. T—Matthew 18:10: "See that you do not despise one of these little ones."

170. T—Matthew 18:11: "For the Son of Man has come to save that which was lost."

171. T—Matthew 18:15: "If your brother sins, go show him his fault in private."

172. T—Matthew 18:16: "But if he does not listen to you, take one or two more with you, so that by the mouth of two or three witnesses every fact may be confirmed."

173. T—Matthew 18:18: "Whatever you will bind on earth shall be bound in heaven; and whatever you loose on earth shall be loosed in heaven."

174. T—Matthew 18:22: The rule for forgiveness is not seven times, but seventy times seven.

175. T—Matthew 18:35: "My heavenly Father will also do the same to you, if each of you does not forgive his brother from your heart."

176. S—Matthew 19:2: He healed great multitudes.

177. T—Matthew 19:9: "Whoever divorces his wife, except for immorality, and marries another woman commits adultery."

178. S—Matthew 19:15: Jesus laid His hands on children and prayed for them.

179. T—Matthew 19:21: "If you wish to be complete, go and sell your possessions and give to the poor, and you will have treasure in heaven; and come, follow Me."

180. T—Matthew 19:29: "Everyone who has left houses or brothers or sisters or father or mother or children or farms for My name's sake will receive many times as much, and shall inherit eternal life."

181. T—Matthew 20:16: "The last shall be first, and the first last."

182. T—Matthew 20:26: "Whoever wishes to become great among you shall be your servant."

183. T—Matthew 20:27: "Whoever wishes to be first among you shall be your slave."

184. T—Matthew 20:28: "The Son of Man did not come to be served, but to serve, and to give His life a ransom for many."

185. S—Matthew 20:34: Moved with compassion, Jesus healed two blind men.

186. S—Matthew 21:12: Jesus cast out all who were buying and selling in the temple.

187. T—Matthew 21:13: "My house shall be called a house of prayer."

188. S—Matthew 21:14: The blind and the lame came to Him in the temple, and He healed them.

189. S—Matthew 21:18: He became hungry.

190. T—Matthew 21:22: "All things you ask in prayer, believing you will receive."

191. S—Matthew 21:23: He was teaching in the temple.

192. T—Matthew 22:21: "Render to Caesar the things that are Caesar's; and to God the things that are God's."

193. S—Matthew 22:33: They were astonished at His teaching.

194. T—Matthew 22:37: "You shall love the Lord your God with all your heart, and with all your soul, and with all your mind."

195. T—Matthew 22:39: "You shall love your neighbor as yourself."

196. T—Matthew 23:1–39: Seven Woes.

197. T—Matthew 24:4: "See to it that no one misleads you."

198. T—Matthew 24:6: "See that you are not frightened."

199. T—Matthew 24:13: "But the one who endures to the end, he will be saved."

200. T—Matthew 24:23: About the antichrist: "Do not believe him."

201. T—Matthew 24:26: About false messiahs and false prophets: "Do not believe them."

202. T—Matthew 24:32: The parable from the fig tree.

203. T—Matthew 24:33: "Recognize that He is near, right at the door."

204. T—Matthew 24:42: "Be on the alert, for you do not know which day your Lord is coming."

205. T—Matthew 24:44: "For this reason you also must be ready."

206. T—Matthew 25:13: "Be on the alert then, for you do not know the day nor the hour."

207. T—Matthew 25:35–36: "For I was hungry , and you gave Me something to eat; I was thirsty, and you gave me something to drink; I was a stranger, and you invited Me in; naked, and you clothed Me; I was sick, and you visited Me; I was in prison, and you came to Me."

208. T—Matthew 26:26–29: Communion.

209. S—Matthew 26:30: Jesus sang a hymn with His disciples.

210. T—Matthew 26:36: "Sit here while I go over there and pray."

211. S—Matthew 26:37: Jesus began to be grieved and distressed.

212. T—Matthew 26:38: "Keep watch with Me."

213. S—Matthew 26:39: He fell on His face and prayed.

214. T—Matthew 26:41: "Keep watching and praying that you may not enter into temptation; the spirit is willing, but the flesh is weak."

215. S—Matthew 26:42: He prayed a second time.

216. S—Matthew 26:44: He prayed a third time.

217. T—Matthew 26:52: "Put your sword back into its place; for all those who take up the sword shall perish by the sword."

218. S—Matthew 26:63: Jesus kept silent.

219. S—Matthew 26:67: They spit in His face and beat Him with their fists, and others slapped Him.

220. T—Matthew 27:11: "It is as you say," in answer to Pilate's question, "Are you the King of the Jews?"

221. S—Matthew 27:12: While He was being accused, He did not answer.

222. S—Matthew 27:14: He did not answer the governor in regard to even a single charge, much to the governor's amazement.

223. T—Matthew 27:46: "My God, My God, why have you forsaken Me?"

224. S—Matthew 27:50: Jesus cried out again with a loud voice, and yielded up His spirit.

225. S—Matthew 28:3: His appearance was like lightning and His garment as white as snow.

226. S—Matthew 28:9: Jesus met the women and greeted them. They took hold of His feet and worshiped Him.

227. T—Matthew 28:10: "Do not be afraid; go and take word to My brethren."

228. T—Matthew 28:19–20: "Go therefore and make disciples of all the nations, baptizing them in the name of the Father and the Son and the Holy Spirit, teaching them to observe all that I commanded you; and lo, I am with you always, even to the end of the age."

GOSPEL GRIT
Mark

As I write *Gospel Grit* for Mark, Luke, and John, I find myself commenting on far fewer verses compared to the ninety-three in Matthew. This is because I referenced like passages in Matthew, ever narrowing what is left in the remaining three books. What that means is that the remaining verses are very special as they are unique to their books.

As you read, keep in mind the posture of Jesus. He is homeless and backpacking His way through the roads of the Middle East, focusing on a very small area of the world. There was nobody taking notes. Jesus was not journaling. Yet somehow, God captured for us, in writing, three of the most amazing years of humanity ever recorded.

In the Gospels, Jesus is giving us instructions on every area of life for every century of life. Jesus is a master on every subject and is able to show us how to follow Him. He shows us how to live for Him. He shows us and tells us what His expectations are for us. He has left a template that transcends time. He has left for us a model that works. Our task is to follow Him.

You may be in an office reading this book. You may be sitting by a crackling fire in the comfort of your home. You may be almost anywhere. Together, you and I are in a twenty-first-century mode of operation. To really capture Jesus, we need to put ourselves in His environment. We are following a man who is becoming more famous by the day, a man who has no address, no job, and no credentials. We are following a man who has, at the most, a backpack filled with a change or two of clothes. He has no books in His possession, no Bible to teach from, no iPad to draw from. He is not able to Google or MapQuest His next city, nor

Facebook his friends. Yet, following Jesus in what He showed us and told us works for every century.

Without further introduction, let's learn some more ways to follow Jesus through the eyes of Mark.

S—MARK 2:8: IMMEDIATELY, JESUS WAS AWARE IN HIS SPIRIT.

(See also Luke 9:47, Luke 11:17, and Luke 20:23; four references.)

Every child some time or another has faked out his parents. I remember a day I played a trick on my mother while coming home from school one warm September afternoon. Back in the old days, we would carry a metal lunch box to school. Of course, we would bring it home with the garbage so Mom could empty it and put something nice in it for the next day at school. One afternoon I got the idea to catch as many grasshoppers as I could while walking down our nearly quarter-mile driveway and use them to fill my lunch box. I was quite successful in capturing most of the population in our area that afternoon. I would like to tell you there were millions in my pail, but that might be an exaggeration. I patiently waited for Mom to open it. Oh, how I laughed when she began to scream. Yet another time I got spanked!

Unlike my mother, Jesus is never caught off guard. I could never fill a backpack with locusts and wait for Him to sit on a rock by the road and end up with a million locusts jumping out of the pack. Why? Because Jesus had the ability to see what was coming.

None of us can outsmart Jesus. We can't fake Him out. None of us can spend the day in rebellion, putting things in our backpack that do not belong in it, without Jesus knowing all about it. Yet, we do stupid things all the time. We need to remember often that Jesus is fully aware of what we are doing, and there is nothing we can hide from Him!

As we walk with Him, following Him, we can never quietly zip open His backpack and secretly play a trick on Jesus. Besides, there is too much at stake to be messing around with the grasshoppers of life!

Gospel Grit Challenge: What might you be doing that truly is a waste of time? What are you doing that is not profitable? What are you picking up that will detour you from really following Jesus all the way? Let it go!

S—MARK 3:1: HE ENTERED AGAIN INTO A SYNAGOGUE.

(See also Mark 11:27; two references.)

Have you noticed that Jesus often went to church? We live in a day when the church is taking a terrible hit. Many people are walking away from it. In this passage, we find Jesus walking to the church. The synagogue was different from what we encounter today, nevertheless, it was church for His day and time. Mark tells us He went there "again"; meaning Jesus was a frequent-flier in the synagogue. Jesus found a reason to go to church. We need to do the same.

Keep in mind the physical appearance of Jesus as He walked through the church doors. I leave to go hunting in two days and will be backpacking through the forest of the Coastal Range with my bow looking for an elk. When I get home, after just a few days, I know what I am going to look like and smell like. That will be after only three days. Jesus was on a *three-year* hike, and I have a feeling He didn't carry toiletries in His backpack. Imagine what He must have looked like walking into the temple!

I attend a church that is open to people who come into our doors, and some look like they have been backpacking for three years. Our people are gracious and kind to those who have less than they may have. Such visitors obviously do not look or smell like the majority of those attending our church services.

Jesus was that person who entered the temple an absolute disaster, yet He was on a mission, and a part of that mission was to be in the synagogue. Think what the religious leaders must have thought. Think what those attending must have thought when they saw a hippie walk through their doors! If you are a rebel, you love this image. If you are refined, you may be struggling with it. Either way, ours is to follow Him!

Gospel Grit Challenge: What keeps people from the "synagogue," the church, today? Next time you are in church, pick out the grungiest person you can find and sit by him or her. Two thousand years ago, you would have been sitting by Jesus in the synagogue!

S—MARK 3:5: HE LOOKED AT THEM WITH ANGER, FOR HE WAS GRIEVED AT THEIR HARDNESS OF HEART.

Hardness of heart is a theme that comes up throughout the Bible, so it is no surprise that Jesus brings up the subject. His reaction to it is not small or insignificant: when you combine anger with grief, you have a formula for a reaction that stretches from one end of an emotional roller coaster to the other.

The absolute worst thing we can do is develop a hard heart that leaves no room for change, no room for improvement, no room for transformation. A hard heart will take us down tracks that are a wreck waiting to happen.

Hard hearts develop slowly over time because neglect takes over. Those with hard hearts do not follow Jesus. Those with hard hearts despise Jesus. Hard hearts are the invention of the devil. We all follow someone in this life; hard hearts follow the enemy. Those willing to have Jesus transform their hearts switch their loyalty from the devil to Jesus Christ. That is the miracle of salvation.

Think with me of all the prejudice directed at Jesus. The religious leaders despised Him for gaining more attention than they received. We do not read anywhere that their hatred stemmed from His homelessness, His vagabond style of living life. No, they hated Him because He turned religion upside down and ousted them from what they thought was their place of honor. If you want to be first, you must be last. If you want to be great, you must become the least. If you want to become rich, you must give it all away. I'll bet they wondered what was in His backpack—another teaching, another miracle, another loaf of bread, or a fish stick!

Gospel Grit Challenge: In your backpack, do you carry any residue of a hardened heart? Is there anything you need Jesus to massage? Is your heart bruised from a relationship? Is your heart broken from disappointment? These are the kinds of events that lead to a hard heart. We need Jesus to help us at this point so we can continue backpacking with Him.

T—MARK 4:24: "TAKE CARE OF WHAT YOU LISTEN TO."

We have all been told that the reason God gave us one mouth and two ears was so we could be good listeners. One of my weaknesses is listening, and I truly wish I were a better listener. I get so concerned about what to say, I fail to listen as I should. I have been told more than once by my loving, darling wife, "You never listen." That is a bit strong, but I suppose there is some truth to it. It's not that Joanie is not talking; it's that I am not listening.

As we walk down the trail with Jesus, picture Him looking back, saying something to us. On the trail we can be busy looking at the scenery, the ground, just about anything and everything. Somehow, we need to be able to listen when Jesus speaks. I am certain He is speaking to us on a regular basis, but I am not so certain we are ready listeners.

We are to follow His voice, His will, and His commands, knowing He will give us clear direction for the moment. He rarely gives us instructions for longer than that. Our task in following Him is not only to keep His backpack in sight but to look for those times He looks over His shoulder and says something to us!

Gospel Grit Challenge: When did you last hear from Jesus? Would you be willing to read His Word more regularly so you can reconnect with Him?

T—MARK 6:4: "A PROPHET IS NOT WITHOUT HONOR EXCEPT IN HIS HOMETOWN AND AMONG HIS OWN RELATIVES AND IN HIS OWN HOUSEHOLD."

Following Jesus is not always easy. In fact, most of what we read in the Gospels shows us that it was a burden for Jesus to walk the roads of Israel.

Rejection is tough to take! We are not wired to enjoy rejection. Mostly, we have to endure it. I never did much dating because I was so afraid of rejection. There were other reasons too, but fear of rejection was at the top of the list.

Probably the single greatest reason Christians do not witness more is fear of rejection. We take the rejection personally even though it is Jesus who is being rejected. If rejection were not an issue, I imagine we would have most all of the world evangelized by now. We remain silent and hide our faith, but Jesus teaches us that to follow Him is to be rejected. Some will say yes to the message, but *many* will say no.

The good news is in those few who will say yes. Think of rejection in baseball terminology. If you strike out seven times out of ten, you make the Hall of Fame. Why? Because you get a hit three times out of ten, and in baseball that is good enough to make it into the Hall of Fame.

I would challenge you to throw your fear of rejection into a side pocket in Jesus's backpack; there's room enough for it.

Gospel Grit Challenge: Identify the last time you were rejected for presenting the good news. If it has been quite a while (I will let you define that), it is time to step up to the plate and start swinging again for Jesus!

T—MARK 7:14: "LISTEN TO ME, ALL OF YOU, AND UNDERSTAND."

There are many things in life I do not understand, and at the top of the list is flying. I have to do it for my job and for some vacation time with my wife. But I do not like to fly. My greatest problem is sitting on the ground thinking there is no way those engines can create enough thrust to lift all this weight off the ground.

Then, when I am up in the air, I wonder what keeps us flying. I think, certainly the weight is more than what the engines can handle for safe travel!

Oddly enough, the only part about flying I like is when the plane starts to go down. I hate turbulence. I pray every time there is turbulence, making sure all my sins are forgiven and all my family is prayed for one last time.

My problem with flying is clearly a lack of understanding. Our problem with Jesus is equally clearly a lack of understanding. If we understood everything He said and everything He was about, we would follow Him over a cliff. Our difficulty with following is that we want it to make sense, and we want life with Jesus to always seem better than what we could do if we weren't following Him.

It isn't enough to listen. Jesus is asking us to *understand* what He tells us and to *imitate* what He shows us. This is what it means to follow Jesus. I have learned that when I do not understand, I need to trust Him until it does make sense. On the days when things do not make sense, I need to trust Him all the more because Jesus always has our best interests in mind.

Gospel Grit Challenge: What doubts do you have about following Jesus? Doubts are a result of a failure to understand. He will not fail you, so take your doubts out of your backpack and put them in His. Put some trust in your bag instead and have a great day!

S—MARK 8:12: HE SIGHED DEEPLY IN HIS SPIRIT.

Think of all the ways Jesus could have ministered for three years to people without having to rough it the way He did. When I go to the mission field, my goal is not to see how miserable I can be to validate the trip. I try to be as comfortable as possible so that I can be more effective! Jesus could have at least had an office space somewhere or a place to cut down the travel from town to town.

On this day when Jesus sighed, He may have been hot, tired, or discouraged. He may have been thinking about His time in heaven and wondering why He left. When I am hot and tired and totally uncomfortable, I tend to sigh too. But Jesus was not sighing because He couldn't find a job, nor because He had no address. Jesus was sighing because the people He came to help were always looking for a miracle. He sighed because they were always looking for signs. He *was* the sign, but they didn't see it.

Are we any different today? We are forever looking for signs from God. Jesus challenges us to follow Him because we love Him, not so we can enjoy another miracle. Jesus challenges us to follow Him because He wants us to enjoy His presence. He desires a relationship with us. In following Him, we develop relationship. The whole point of this life and the life to come is to be with Jesus!

Gospel Grit Challenge: Is Jesus enough for you? Are you satisfied with Jesus? Prove it!

T—MARK 8:38: "FOR WHOEVER IS ASHAMED OF ME AND MY WORDS IN THIS ADULTEROUS AND SINFUL GENERATION, THE SON OF MAN WILL ALSO BE ASHAMED OF HIM WHEN HE COMES IN THE GLORY OF HIS FATHER WITH THE HOLY ANGELS."

First, let's recognize the times in which we live. We live in a sinful and adulterous generation. If it was true in Jesus's day, it is even more so in our day. Jesus is teaching us to not be so concerned about what others think and to be more concerned about what He thinks.

Peer pressure is real, and most of the time it's tough to handle. We want so badly to please and impress others that it may affect following Jesus.

Jesus had the knowledge of who He really was. He was homeless, but He was also the Son of God! He knew His hiking days were to be short-lived. Likewise, Jesus wants us to understand that our hike through this life is short compared to our time in eternity. Because of the brevity of life, we are told to take a stand for Jesus in the midst of a people who are not taking a stand for Him.

Our challenge is not to fixate on the here and now as much as on the then and later, when we will be in the presence of Jesus. May God help us to recognize that the hike we are on in this life is temporary and brief. It is more important to impress Jesus than people!

Gospel Grit Challenge: Are you influenced, or do you influence? Are you led, or do you lead? Find ways to not be ashamed of following Jesus Christ.

S—MARK 9:2: HE TOOK PETER, JAMES, AND JOHN UP TO A HIGH MOUNTAIN BY THEMSELVES.

Children love special times with their father or mother. Many times my dad would take me golfing as a teenager, and those Saturdays were special for me. I remember them with great fondness.

Jesus has extended His invitation to each of us to hike up the mountain with Him. If you have ever hiked up a steep trail and reached the summit, you know the lookout can be spectacular. Such is the case where I live in the heart of the Cascade Mountain Range. The views are magnificent.

Jesus offers us a spectacular view if we follow Him. However, while the views are magnificent, so is the journey getting there! I will be hiking steep mountains over the next several days as I hunt for the elusive Roosevelt elk. I know there will be times when I will be exhausted, and stopping to rest, taking off my pack and enjoying the scenery, will be rewarding. This is what Jesus offers you and me. The summit is magnificent, but so is the company we keep getting there. This is what following Jesus is all about; it's just spending time with Him.

Gospel Grit Challenge: When was the last time you took a break and just sat and talked with Jesus? Has He taken you up any trails lately?

Remember, the summit is rewarding in part because the climb is so difficult. Don't give up now on following Jesus; you may be only days away from the summit.

T—MARK 9:23: "'IF YOU CAN'? ALL THINGS ARE POSSIBLE TO HIM WHO BELIEVES."

I was a junior in high school, playing in the club championship at Top O' Scott Golf Course. I had been raised to go to church and not to play golf on Sundays. This particular weekend, it was a two-day tournament. I was tied for the lead going into the second day. After three holes I was two under par, leading the tournament. Upon walking up the fourth fairway, I looked at my watch and noticed it was eleven o'clock. Any other Sunday, I would have been in church. Our church always began the service with a song that included the words, "Only believe, all things are possible, only believe." I longed to be in church as I played that song through my head, so I told my playing partners I was withdrawing from the tournament because being in church worshiping God was of greater value than winning a golf tournament.

I walked to my car, got in, and drove to church. Was it wrong for me to play golf that particular Sunday? No! I just wanted to be in church! It was that song, based on this teaching from Jesus, that caused me to follow Jesus in a direction I was not expecting that day. I made the right choice.

Gospel Grit Challenge: Is there anything you are doing that may require reversing direction and following Jesus to a better place than the golf course?

T—MARK 9:50: "HAVE SALT IN YOURSELVES, AND BE AT PEACE WITH ONE ANOTHER."

(See also John 20:19, John 20:21, and John 20:26; four references.)

The word that captures my attention in these verses is "peace." I value peace above most other feelings in my life.

When I am not at peace, I am miserable. When I am not at peace with God, I am even more miserable. It is strange to think my peace comes from a guy who probably wore a shaggy beard, worn-out clothes, and a backpack so dirty it would be impossible to figure out what color it was originally. None of that matters to me, and it should not matter to you. I do not care what Jesus looks like or smells like so long as He can give me peace. He can give me a whole lot more too, but peace is priceless. Peace allows us to sleep, to function, to live with less stress. Peace allows us to think clearly. Peace allows us to enjoy life. Peace is huge! Jesus is the giver of peace.

Following Jesus puts us on the trail to peace. If you lack peace, I urge you to get within eyesight of that dirty old backpack, because the guy in front of us is Jesus Christ. His backpack is filled with peace!

Gospel Grit Challenge: Get back to Jesus. Get back to the Word. Get back to really following Jesus, and you will find peace. What steps do you need to take today to get started?

T—MARK 12:30–31: "'YOU SHALL LOVE THE LORD YOUR GOD WITH ALL YOUR HEART, AND WITH ALL YOUR SOUL, AND WITH ALL YOUR MIND, AND WITH ALL YOUR STRENGTH.' THE SECOND IS THIS, 'YOU SHALL LOVE YOUR NEIGHBOR AS YOURSELF.' THERE IS NO OTHER COMMANDMENT GREATER THAN THESE."

(See also John 15:14; two references.)

This passage on loving God with our entire being takes it one step further than Matthew did. Not only does Mark add "strength" to the list of things with which to love God, we are told by Jesus to love our neighbor to the extent that we love ourselves.

Some neighbors are easier to love than other neighbors. We live in a great neighborhood. A few years back, new neighbors moved in next door to us who loved to party until almost sunrise on Sunday mornings. The music was loud, the drinking was obsessive, and cars were everywhere. We dreaded summers.

One night two guys got mad at each other and began fighting. At one point one of them pulled out a butcher knife and started chasing the other guy around on our street. To make matters worse, they had three pit bulls. I could write a chapter just on our experiences with their dogs. Loving these neighbors was a tall order.

Honestly, we were friendly to them and they were friendly to us, but I never did share Jesus with them. Sometimes loving our neighbors means we take the high road when we would love to see them living somewhere else. Other times Jesus demands we share His love with them. I suppose I could have done a better job of loving my neighbor. I just want you to see that some days it is hard to do what Jesus asks. I suppose I could have gotten a dog biscuit out of Jesus's backpack!

Gospel Grit Challenge: Are there any neighbors living near you whom you can be a better witness to?

T—MARK 13:29: "WHEN YOU SEE THESE THINGS HAPPENING, RECOGNIZE THAT HE IS NEAR."

This is an exciting teaching because of the implications of being with Jesus on the other side of eternity. Today we follow a Savior who was fully man under the worst of circumstances. When He comes to get us and take us to heaven, we will follow a Savior who is fully man under the best of circumstances.

Following Jesus as described in the Bible is awesome, but following Him around heaven is going to be even more awesome. He will have flowing robes of righteousness and be wearing the clothes of a king! He will not have a backpack on his shoulders; there will be children riding on His shoulders instead.

That old backpack filled with our problems will be cast out of heaven. (The good things we carried—like love, joy, and peace—we get to keep.) It's even possible that Jesus kicks that old backpack filled with nothing but problems, sorrows, and sadness all the way to hell and some demon picks it up and gives it to his boss to wear!

As you follow Jesus today, fill your mind with thoughts of actually seeing Him soon!

Gospel Grit Challenge: How many times a day do you think about seeing Jesus face-to-face? Start doing this exercise today. Remember, for now we follow Him and can see only the backpack on His back. Soon we shall see Him face-to-face!

S—MARK 14:33: HE BEGAN TO BE VERY DISTRESSED AND TROUBLED.

Why was Jesus becoming distressed and troubled? Jesus knew His three years of ministry were about to come to an end, but that isn't what bothered Him. He would be glad to finish that journey. But He knew what the trade-in would be for the backpack. He was thinking of the one event left in His life on earth, the event that would change the world.

Jesus was fixated on the cross from this point forward. As we follow Him, we do not take a detour while He goes to the cross. We are to follow Him even there. We love Easter and Resurrection Sunday. We love the empty tomb. But for the tomb to have meaning, there must be a tragedy that takes place. Jesus was about to become the victim of the tragedy.

We must recognize that every trip has a beginning and an ending. Jesus was about to reach the end of His three-year journey with His followers. Why? So He could have many more followers than what those three years had given Him. Today you and I are His followers. We must follow Him to the cross so others can join us in following Him as well.

Be looking for people who are putting on backpacks. They just received Jesus and have begun their journey with Him. Show them how to best follow Jesus. Teach them all you can about the importance of the backpack—of what we put in there and what we throw out. Help them not to worry about things like a job or where to live and instead focus solely on following Jesus.

Gospel Grit Challenge: Look for someone who is a new follower of Jesus Christ or is just getting serious about Him again after a time away. Who can you help who is new to the faith?

S—MARK 16:14: HE REPROACHED THEM FOR THEIR UNBELIEF AND HARDNESS OF HEART.

This passage is not like the other passages on hard hearts and unbelief. It is different on several levels.

First, these men had been with Jesus for three years and had followed Him everywhere. They knew He had no money yet had the ability to feed five thousand people at a time and provide leftovers. They knew He had no home yet had promised them mansions for following Him. They knew He was a backpacking vagabond yet had performed miracle after miracle before their very eyes.

These men knew who Jesus was. He was not your typical tourist on a Holy Land tour. He needed no earthly guide. He was God. Jesus told them what would happen, and it happened just the way He said it would. Yet they still doubted.

Jesus told them He was going to die, and they watched Him die. Jesus told them He would rise from the dead, and He did. If anyone should recognize Him, it would be these guys!

They trusted Jesus. They gave up homes to follow Jesus. They knew better, yet they doubted. May God help us who have been backpacking with Jesus not only through the streets and towns of Israel but through the cities of all the countries of the world, wherever followers of Jesus Christ are found, to be found faithful and true to Jesus Christ.

Gospel Grit Challenge: List the evidences that Jesus is God in your life. He has been faithful to you. Keep following Him, no matter what!

Scriptures from Mark
for Further Study

229. S—Mark 1:12: Immediately the Spirit impelled Him to go out into the wilderness.
230. S—Mark 1:14: He preached the gospel of God.
231. T—Mark 1:15: "Repent and believe in the gospel."
232. T—Mark 1:17: "Follow Me and I will make you become fishers of men."
233. S—Mark 1:20: Immediately He called them; they left their nets and followed Him.
234. S—Mark 1:21: He entered the synagogue and began to preach.
235. S—Mark 1:25: Jesus cast out an unclean spirit.
236. S—Mark 1:31: Jesus healed Peter's mother-in-law of a fever.
237. S—Mark 1:34: He healed many who were ill with various diseases and cast out many demons.
238. S—Mark 1:35: Early in the morning while still dark, He went alone to pray.
239. T—Mark 1:38: "Let us go to the towns so that I may preach there."
240. S—Mark 1:39: He preached in the synagogues and cast out demons.
241. S—Mark 1:41: He was moved with compassion.
242. S—Mark 1:41: He cleansed a man with leprosy.
243. T—Mark 1:44: "Show yourself to the priest and offer for your cleansing what Moses commanded."
244. S—Mark 2:2: He was speaking the word to them.
245. S—Mark 2:5: Seeing their faith, Jesus forgave sin.
246. S—Mark 2:8: Immediately, Jesus was aware in His spirit.
247. S—Mark 2:11: Jesus had authority to forgive sins—He physically healed a paralytic.
248. S—Mark 2:13: He was teaching them.
249. T—Mark 2:14: "Follow Me!"
250. S—Mark 2:15: He ate with many sinners.

251. T—Mark 2:17: "I did not come to call the righteous, but sinners."
252. S—Mark 3:1: He entered again into a synagogue.
253. S—Mark 3:5: He looked at them with anger, for He was grieved at their hardness of heart.
254. S—Mark 3:5: He healed the man's hand.
255. S—Mark 3:7: Jesus withdrew to the sea with His disciples.
256. S—Mark 3:10: He healed many.
257. S—Mark 3:13: He went up to the mountains and summoned those whom He Himself wanted.
258. S—Mark 3:14–15: And He appointed twelve, that they might be with Him, and that He might send them out to preach, and to have authority to cast out demons.
259. S—Mark 3:20: He came home.
260. S—Mark 3:23: He began speaking to them in parables.
261. T—Mark 3:29: "Whoever blasphemes against the Holy Spirit never has forgiveness, but is guilty of an eternal sin."
262. T—Mark 3:35: "For whoever does the will of God, he is My brother and sister and mother."
263. S—Mark 4:1: He began to teach again by the sea.
264. S—Mark 4:2: He was teaching them many things in parables.
265. T—Mark 4:9: "He who has ears to hear, let him hear."
266. S—Mark 4:10: As soon as He was alone, His followers, along with the twelve, began asking questions about the parables.
267. T—Mark 4:24: "Take care of what you listen to."
268. S—Mark 4:33: With many such parables He spoke the word to them as they were able to hear it.
269. S—Mark 4:34: He did not speak to them without a parable.
270. S—Mark 4:34: He explained everything privately to His own disciples.
271. S—Mark 4:36: And He left the multitude.
272. S—Mark 4:38: He was in the stern, asleep on the cushion.
273. T—Mark 4:39: He rebuked the wind and said to the sea, "Hush, be still."
274. T—Mark 5:8: "Come out of the man, you unclean spirit."

275. S—Mark 5:30: Jesus immediately perceived that the power proceeding from Him had gone forth.

276. T—Mark 5:36: "Do not be afraid any longer, only believe."

277. S—Mark 5:41–42: Jesus brought a twelve-year-old girl back to life.

278. S—Mark 6:2: He began to teach in the synagogue.

279. T—Mark 6:4: "A prophet is not without honor except in his hometown and among his own relatives and in his own household."

280. S—Mark 6:5: He could do no miracle there except that He laid His hands on a few sick people and healed them.

281. S—Mark 6:6: He went around the villages teaching.

282. S—Mark 6:7–9: He summoned the twelve and began to send them out in pairs. He gave them authority over the unclean spirits and instructed them to take nothing for their journey, except a staff—no bread, no bag, no money in their belt.

283. T—Mark 6:10–11: "Wherever you enter a house, stay there until you leave town. Any place that does not receive you or listen to you, as you go out from there, shake the dust off the soles of your feet for a testimony against them."

284. T—Mark 6:31: "Come away by yourselves to a secluded place and rest a while."

285. S—Mark 6:34: He felt compassion for them.

286. S—Mark 6:34: He began to teach them many things.

287. T—Mark 6:37: "You give them something to eat."

288. S—Mark 6:41: Looking up toward heaven, He blessed the food and broke the loaves, and He kept giving them to the disciples.

289. S—Mark 6:46: He departed to the mountain to pray.

290. S—Mark 6:48: He came to them walking on the sea.

291. T—Mark 6:50: "Take courage; it is I, do not be afraid."

292. T—Mark 7:14: "Listen to Me, all of you, and understand."

293. S—Mark 7:17: After leaving the multitude, He entered the house.

294. T—Mark 7:20: "That which proceeds out of the man, that is what defiles the man."

295. S—Mark 7:29: He cast a demon out of a daughter.

296. S—Mark 7:33: He took him aside from the multitude by himself.

297. S—Mark 7:34: He looked up to heaven.

298. T—Mark 8:2: "I feel compassion for the people because they have remained with Me now three days and have nothing to eat."

299. S—Mark 8:6: He gave thanks and broke the loaves and started giving them to His disciples to serve the multitude.

300. S—Mark 8:7: After He blessed the fish, He had them served as well.

301. S—Mark 8:12: He sighed deeply in His spirit.

302. S—Mark 8:13: He left them.

303. T—Mark 8:15: "Watch out! Beware of the leaven of the Pharisees and the leaven of Herod."

304. S—Mark 8:23: He spit on the blind man's eyes and laid His hands on him.

305. S—Mark 8:25: Again, He laid His hands on the man's eyes.

306. S—Mark 8:27: He questioned His disciples.

307. S—Mark 8:29: He continued to question them.

308. S—Mark 8:30: He warned them to tell no one about Him.

309. S—Mark 8:31: He began to teach them.

310. T—Mark 8:34–35: "If anyone wishes to come after Me, he must deny himself, and take up his cross and follow Me. For whoever wishes to save his life will lose it, but whoever loses his life for My sake and the gospel's will save it."

311. T—Mark 8:38: "For whoever is ashamed of Me and My words in this adulterous and sinful generation, the Son of Man will also be ashamed of him when He comes in the glory of His Father with the holy angels."

312. S—Mark 9:2: He took Peter, James, and John up to a high mountain by themselves.

313. T—Mark 9:23: "'If you can'? All things are possible to him who believes."

314. S—Mark 9:25: He rebuked the unclean spirit.

315. S—Mark 9:27: Jesus took him by the hand and raised him, and he got up.

316. T—Mark 9:29: "This kind cannot come out by anything but prayer."

317. S—Mark 9:31: He was teaching His disciples.

318. T—Mark 9:35: "If anyone wants to be first, he shall be last of all and servant of all."

319. S—Mark 9:36: He took a child in His arms.

320. T—Mark 9:37: "Whoever receives one child like this in My name receives Me; and whoever receives Me does not receive Me, but Him who sent Me."

321. T—Mark 9:50: "Have salt in yourselves, and be at peace with one another."

322. S—Mark 10:1: He once more began to teach them.

323. T—Mark 10:9: "What therefore God has joined together, let no man separate."

324. T—Mark 10:11–12: "Whoever divorces his wife and marries another woman commits adultery against her; and if she herself divorces her husband and marries another man, she is committing adultery."

325. S—Mark 10:13–14: Jesus was indignant when the disciples tried to turn the children away.

326. T—Mark 10:15: "Whoever does not receive the kingdom of God like a child will not enter it at all."

327. S—Mark 10:16: He took the children in His arms and began blessing them, laying His hands on them.

328. S—Mark 10:21: Jesus felt a love for the rich young man.

329. T—Mark 10:21: "One thing you lack: go and sell all you possess and give to the poor, and you will have treasure in heaven; and come, follow Me."

330. T—Mark 10:23: "How hard it will be for those who are wealthy to enter the kingdom of God!"

331. T—Mark 10:31: "Many who are first will be last, and the last, first."

332. S—Mark 10:32: Again He took the twelve aside.

333. T—Mark 10:45: "For even the Son of Man did not come to be served, but to serve, and to give His life a ransom for many."

334. S—Mark 10:52: Jesus heals blind Bartimaeus.

335. S—Mark 11:12: He became hungry.

336. S—Mark 11:15–16: He entered the temple and began to cast out those who were buying and selling there. He overturned the tables of the moneychangers and the seats of those who were selling doves. He would not permit anyone to carry goods through the temple.

337. T—Mark 11:17: "My house shall be called a house of prayer for all the nations. But you have made it a robbers' den."

338. T—Mark 11:22: "Have faith in God."

339. T—Mark 11:24: "All things for which you pray and ask, believe that you have received them, and they will be granted to you."

340. T—Mark 11:25: "Whenever you stand praying, forgive, if you have anything against anyone, so that your Father who is in heaven will also forgive you your transgressions."

341. T—Mark 11:26: "But if you do not forgive, neither will your Father who is in heaven forgive your transgressions."

342. S—Mark 11:27: He was walking in the temple.

343. S—Mark 12:1: He began to speak to them in parables.

344. S—Mark 12:14: You are truthful, and defer to no one; for You are not partial to any, but teach the way of God in truth.

345. T—Mark 12:17: "Render to Caesar the things that are Caesar's, and to God the things that are God's."

346. T—Mark 12:30–31: "'You shall love the Lord your God with all your heart, and with all your soul, and with all your mind, and with all your strength.' The second is this, 'You shall love your neighbor as yourself.' There is no other commandment greater than these."

347. S—Mark 12:35: He taught in the temple.

348. S—Mark 12:37: The crowds enjoyed listening to Him.

349. T—Mark 12:38: "Beware of the Scribes."

350. S—Mark 12:41: He sat down opposite the treasury and began observing how the people were putting money into the treasury.

351. T—Mark 13:5: "See to it that no one misleads you."

352. T—Mark 13:7: "When you hear of wars and rumors of wars, do not be frightened."

353. T—Mark 13:9: "Be on your guard."

354. T—Mark 13:11: "Do not worry beforehand about what you are to say, but say whatever is given you in that hour; for it is not you who speak, but it is the Holy Spirit."

355. T—Mark 13:13: "The one who endures to the end, he will be saved."

356. T—Mark 13:21: "If anyone says to you, 'Behold here is Christ'… do not believe him."

357. T—Mark 13:23: "Take heed."

358. T—Mark 13:28: "Now learn the parable from the fig tree."

359. T—Mark 13:29: "When you see these things happening, recognize that He is near."

360. T—Mark 13:33: "Take heed, keep on the alert."

361. T—Mark 13:35: "Therefore, be on the alert."

362. T—Mark 13:37: "Be on the alert!"

363. S—Mark 14:17: When it was evening He came with the twelve.

364. S—Mark 14:22: He took some bread, and after a blessing He broke it; and gave it to them.

365. T—Mark 14:22: "Take it; this is My body."

366. S—Mark 14:23: When He had taken the cup, and given thanks, He gave it to them; and they all drank from it.

367. T—Mark 14:32: "Sit here until I have prayed."

368. S—Mark 14:33: He began to be very distressed and troubled.

369. T—Mark 14:34: "My soul is deeply grieved to the point of death; remain here and keep watch."

370. S—Mark 14:35: He fell to the ground and began to pray.

371. T—Mark 14:36: "Yet not what I will, but what You will."

372. T—Mark 14:38: "Keep watching and praying that you may not come into temptation; the spirit is willing, but the flesh is weak."

373. S—Mark 14:39: Again He went away and prayed the same words.

374. S—Mark 14:61: He kept silent and gave no answer.

375. S—Mark 15:5: Jesus made no further answer; Pilate was amazed.

376. S—Mark 15:37: Jesus uttered a loud cry, and breathed His last.

377. S—Mark 16:9: He first appeared to Mary Magdalene, from whom He had cast out seven demons.

378. S—Mark 16:14: He reproached them for their unbelief and hardness of heart.
379. T—Mark 16:15: "Go into all the world and preach the gospel to all creation."

Luke

Luke offers more pieces to the puzzle of how to best follow Jesus. Each of the four authors of the Gospels captures things the other three do not. As a physician turned author and follower of Jesus Christ, Luke has a keen set of ears and eyes.

I have a friend who is a physician who likes to backpack through Europe. It is not unreasonable to imagine people from all backgrounds and careers strapping on a backpack and following Jesus. I am sure my friend would have loved an opportunity to follow Jesus around the trails of Israel!

> S—LUKE 2:46: WHEN HE WAS ABOUT TWELVE YEARS OLD, HIS PARENTS FOUND HIM IN THE TEMPLE, SITTING IN THE MIDST OF THE TEACHERS, BOTH LISTENING TO THEM AND ASKING THEM QUESTIONS.

(See also Luke 2:49, Luke 2:51, Luke 2:52, and Luke 3:23; five references.)

These five passages are important because they capture most of Jesus's time on earth, about eighteen of His thirty-three years. They begin with His childhood and His eagerness to be in the temple learning from the religious leaders. These passages speak of Jesus's obedience to His parents and His growth in wisdom and stature and favor with God and with men. The fifth passage tells us the age Jesus began His ministry.

If you are older than thirty, think back to being thirty years of age. If you are younger, think forward to what you will be doing for a living. Walk in the shoes of Jesus and imagine His thoughts as His life was about to make a dramatic shift toward suffering and rejection.

His earlier years were foundational for Jesus, preparing Him for the three most grueling years of His short life. I believe God was preparing Jesus for the extraordinary. I believe that as we follow Jesus, He is always preparing us for the extraordinary.

I was called to preach as a child, and I pursued that calling throughout high school and college and then seminary. I always knew what I wanted to do and looked forward with great anticipation to being a pastor.

Jesus knew from childhood what He was going to be and pursued that throughout His upbringing. However, He also knew His career would be short and painful. He knew His career would be filled with suffering and rejection. Yet He pursued His calling. He knew that within three years of ministry to Israel, they would kill Him. This sounds much like the potential fate of some of our homeless and unemployed in the inner cities of this country. No wonder Jesus made such great attempts to reach the poor, the outcast, and the downtrodden—He was one of them!

Gospel Grit Challenge: Thank Jesus for what He did for you knowing where His career path would take Him. Now, really, thank Him! Now, really, follow Him!

T—LUKE 7:23: "BLESSED IS HE WHO DOES NOT TAKE OFFENSE AT ME."

How would you like to have a job description that requires you to tell the establishment they are wrong and you are right, even though you are unemployed and have few places to take a shower or get cleaned up? Those are the shoes Jesus walked in constantly. He certainly was at a disadvantage.

Yet, Jesus turned the established religious world inside out. He turned religious leaders upside down and ticked a lot of people off. I wonder if sometimes His disciples were more like bodyguards.

His words were offensive to some. His cross and His life offended many. He told us people would hate Him and they would hate us because of Him. He guaranteed it! It is not popular today to tell people they are sinners, and it was not popular then either. That is just never a popular message!

Jesus talked much about money, which was pretty bold considering He was broke and had not held a job since age thirty! Jesus told rich people they were probably going to hell. No wonder they hated Him.

Jesus was never invited to a conference to speak; He was never invited to be the keynote speaker at a religious convention. Jesus spent most of His time with His disciples and with sinners. Jesus had invitations to spend time with sinners, but never the religious elite.

Jesus is telling us we are blessed if we will welcome His teaching and life. Our calling as followers is to never be offended, but to be affected by the One who wears the dusty backpack.

Gospel Grit Challenge: Being told we are wrong is usually offensive. How can you best respond to Scripture that reproves your behavior?

T—LUKE 8:18: "SO TAKE CARE HOW YOU LISTEN; FOR WHOEVER HAS, TO HIM MORE SHALL BE GIVEN; AND WHOEVER DOES NOT HAVE, EVEN WHAT HE THINKS HE HAS SHALL BE TAKEN AWAY FROM HIM."

We have already looked at Jesus's teachings for us on listening. He is now telling us a principle behind listening. Every person following Jesus has something. When we are handed our backpack at conversion, everybody has something inside to start with. How we respond to Jesus as we follow Him determines what stays in the pack, what is added to the pack, and what is taken out of the pack. It all has to do with listening, which has everything to do with obedience.

We live in a culture and a political climate that is polarized over what our future as Americans should be. One philosophy extols big government and fewer liberties. The other philosophy extols limited government and unlimited liberties. The former advocates for unearned equality, while the latter bases what one has on what one does.

Jesus in this passage is teaching His followers to listen up, follow closely, and obey, because there are rewards to be gained and rewards to be lost. Jesus does not advocate for equal distribution. Rather, quite the opposite. The reality in following Jesus is that some will follow really closely, and others will not. There will be an impact on our backpacks either way.

I urge you to follow Jesus closely so that you might gain the greater reward!

Gospel Grit Challenge: Is your cup half-empty or half-full? Obedience to Jesus will lead to a cup filled up and spilling over the side. Disobedience to Jesus will lead to a cup that has a leak in the bottom and loses everything. What's in your cup?

T—LUKE 11:23: "HE WHO IS NOT WITH ME IS AGAINST ME; AND HE WHO DOES NOT GATHER WITH ME, SCATTERS."

I love these types of passages because they are all or nothing. I love black and white. I like it when the answer is either yes or no. I do not do well with maybe answers. When someone tells me they will get back to me, I get frustrated.

I remember the day I asked my girlfriend to marry me. Had she told me she would get back to me on that one, I would have given up altogether. Even if her answer was no, I would have at least known where I stood. Thankfully her answer was yes. We have been married for almost thirty-two years.

Following Jesus requires a yes or a no answer. Following Jesus is not like a light switch relationship, one day on and another day off. The problem is, many people live this way and say they are following Jesus. Following Jesus is not like a faucet, where one moment the water is flowing and the next moment the water stops. Following Jesus is like a flowing river. Some days it has the current leading up to Niagara Falls. Other days it is like a hot, humid, summer afternoon on the lazy Mississippi River. However, the river is always flowing!

Following Jesus was never meant to be stagnant or boring. Following Jesus was meant to be rich and rewarding.

Gospel Grit Challenge: Jesus was unemployed in the world's eyes. There is nothing quite as exciting as hearing the words, "You are hired." And there is nothing quite as deflating as hearing the words, "You are fired." Fortunately, Jesus is hiring—and it's a full-time position. Are you ready to report for duty?

T—LUKE 11:35: "THEN WATCH OUT THAT THE LIGHT IN YOU IS NOT DARKNESS."

I am always concerned when I read passages like this one. I would like to think I am following Jesus closely, and I hope you are too. Nonetheless, we must heed His warning. Apparently on the trail of life there are dangerous parts of the road where, if we are not walking in His footsteps, we can get hurt.

Though I teach at a university part-time, I never have liked exams. They make me anxious, so I show much grace to my students in this area. Jesus asks us to always examine everything against Scripture. Scripture becomes our compass for any direction we go in life.

If you think you are hearing God's voice, I would urge you to match it up against Scripture. If what you are hearing or planning is not squared with Scripture, then you know this verse is a caution for your life. Not a threat, just a serious caution. Following Jesus means following His Word.

Gospel Grit Challenge: Are you filling up daily with passages from the Bible? If not, what will it take for you to start filling up at the pump? Have you examined the things you believe you are hearing or are planning to do in the light of Scripture?

> T—LUKE 12:5: "BUT I WILL WARN YOU WHOM TO FEAR: FEAR THE ONE WHO, AFTER HE HAS KILLED, HAS AUTHORITY TO CAST INTO HELL; YES, I TELL YOU, FEAR HIM!"

This one is tricky. It's a jolt. This unassuming, backpacking guy is now not so mild-mannered anymore. In this teaching, we are seeing the divine in Jesus coming out! In this passage, Jesus is asserting His authority and making sure everyone knows who is in charge.

Sometimes it's hard to know how to relate to God. On the one hand, we are told to fear Him. On the other hand, we are told *not* to fear Him. Which is it? We are to fear God in that we are not to be flippant toward Him. We are not to fear Him in that we are His children, and when children are following what their parents tell them to do, then they know all is well. We only need to fear when we are living in disobedience.

Jesus is making it clear that if we do not follow after Him, there will be eternal consequences. Again, Jesus is not being gray. Jesus is drawing a line in the Galilean sand and telling us we have a choice. I am choosing to follow very closely to Jesus; how about you?

Gospel Grit Challenge: Do you ever think about hell? Does hell scare you? Should hell scare you? Where do people who do not follow Jesus go after they die? Should you be thinking about hell more in your day? If yes, how would it make your day different?

> T—LUKE 14:11: "FOR EVERYONE WHO EXALTS HIMSELF WILL BE HUMBLED, AND HE WHO HUMBLES HIMSELF WILL BE EXALTED.""

A God who chooses to be unemployed and homeless is about as humble as anyone could get. We do not ever read of Jesus having luggage tied onto a camel. In fact, the only time we read of Jesus riding an animal at all, it is a donkey, and that for only a short trip. For being the Son of God, Jesus is the epitome of humility.

Jesus never exalted Himself. Exalting Jesus is the responsibility of His followers. What an awesome privilege to exalt King Jesus in this life and in the life to come! Our primary task as His followers in heaven will be to exalt Him forever and ever.

The most humiliating death in Jesus's day was death on a cross. Jesus chose the path of humility at every turn. Humility is a tough one, because our culture teaches us to think and do otherwise. In fact, our culture elevates man to be equal with or above God. That is the goal of humanism. That is the goal of progressive liberalism. The goal is to elevate the accomplishments of man at the expense of God. Every time God is excluded, man is elevated.

The only thing worse than pride is false humility—people who claim to be humble, yet deny God. Anything good that happens, all glory and praise and honor is to go to Jesus Christ. Any portion that goes to us goes to our heads, and we swell up with pride. Indeed, we need to take this teaching to heart. Jesus taught it, and more importantly, He showed us humility.

Gospel Grit Challenge: Think of ways to dismantle pride. Think of ways to incorporate humility in your life. Think of someone who is very prideful, and try not to be like them. Think of someone who is humble, and spend as much time with them as you can.

T—LUKE 16:9: "MAKE FRIENDS FOR YOURSELVES BY MEANS OF THE WEALTH OF UNRIGHTEOUSNESS, SO THAT WHEN IT FAILS, THEY WILL RECEIVE YOU INTO ETERNAL DWELLINGS."

This is a powerful teaching on things that last and things that do not last. Wealth does not last. We strive so hard to accumulate it our entire lives, only to leave it all when we die. Missionaries are forced to sell most everything they own to go to the mission field. We feel sorry for them because they have so little. Actually, we probably feel guilty because we have more than what we should own.

My dad had a conversation with me about a year ago about what would happen to all of his things when he died. It dawned on him that I was going to sell all of it! Things that mean so much to us usually mean little to others, even family. I encouraged Dad to sell his stuff or give it away while he still had the ability to do so.

You and I have the ability to scale things down if we choose. The real question is not how much we possess. The question is, what do we have in our backpack? Whatever is in there is probably what we value most. We are to use the tools of this world to prepare our lives for the world that is to come. Jesus is teaching us to be resourceful, because in the end, we are not taking even a backpack to heaven.

For the next three days I will be hunting in the woods with a single backpack. I assure you I have in that pack only the things that will ensure the likelihood of me surviving in the woods for three days. Why? Because I want to live beyond this wild adventure I am about to embark on. So it is with eternity: the things of this world are but tools to help us make it to the next!

Gospel Grit Challenge: Think of ways you can detach from the things of this world. Now, think of ways you can attach yourself to eternity. Be very specific!

T—LUKE 17:32: "REMEMBER LOT'S WIFE."

Of all the things Jesus brings up from the past, this example may be the most bizarre. Jesus is enjoying campfires, fish fries, and toying with the religious leaders. He is strolling through Israel with a band of followers like Forrest Gump on his run across America. Then, out of the blue, Jesus tells us to remember the tragic story of a rather obscure character from what was, even then, a long time ago.

To remember Lot's wife is to remember what she did that caused Jesus to make this reference to her. Lot's wife was told specifically to *not look back,* and if she did look back, she would become the mate to a pepper shaker! Sure enough, she looked back.

Jesus wants us to keep our eyes on Him, and He is always forward looking. If we look back, like the Hebrew people, we may find ourselves longing to be slaves again just because life in Egypt is familiar. Jesus is always taking us into new territory. If there was no new territory there would be no need to trust Him, to have faith in Him, or to rely upon Him. Jesus does not want us to set up shop and get comfy and familiar with life; rather, He wants us to be mobile and ready to serve where needed.

While being homeless or unemployed are not desired by most, there are some advantages. I had to get up at 5 a.m. to go to work today, and I have appointments all day. I have utility bills to pay and a house payment to make, and I must keep my job to keep my house. With these things come stress and worry. Jesus is teaching us about responsibility and obedience. He wants us to be so unattached to things that following Him is a joy, not a burden!

Gospel Grit Challenge: What do you find yourself looking back at in life that you wish you still had? What steps do you need to take to ensure you look forward and keep following Jesus and are not sidetracked by something or someone from the past?

T—LUKE 18:27: "THE THINGS THAT ARE IMPOSSIBLE WITH PEOPLE ARE POSSIBLE WITH GOD."

This study has shown many reasons why following Jesus is the best way to live. This teaching may be at the top of the list. The bottom line in this life is there are things man cannot do. Likewise, there are things only God can do. In fact, Jesus teaches us that nothing is impossible with God.

When I was younger I used to think most everything was possible because I was young, seemingly invincible, and able to make it through the day without much sleep. My, how things have changed now that I am in my fifties! While my physical capabilities continue to shrink, my perspective on God continues to expand. More and more, I see that nothing is impossible with Him.

I have a word of encouragement for anyone reading this book who may be unemployed: God is able to supply you with a job. But you must follow Jesus so that you can hear His voice telling you where to get the job. If you are about to lose your home on a foreclosure or a short sale, God is able to keep a roof over your head. Following Jesus means trusting Jesus. Following Jesus means doing things His way. Following Jesus may mean a budget that is more frugal than what you are used to. Following Jesus and living in a one-bedroom apartment is better than not following Jesus and living in a mansion!

The point Jesus makes is simple: everything is possible with God! With that truth in our backpack, why would we follow anyone else but Jesus?

Gospel Grit Challenge: Write down the miracle you are in need of today, remembering that with God, all things are possible.

T—LUKE 19:26: "I TELL YOU THAT TO EVERYONE WHO HAS, MORE SHALL BE GIVEN, BUT FROM THE ONE WHO DOES NOT HAVE, EVEN WHAT HE DOES HAVE SHALL BE TAKEN AWAY."

I am fully aware that a verse like this was addressed earlier in this study, but I felt it beneficial to look at this teaching again. Have you ever wondered why there is so much repetition in the Gospels? I have. And have you ever wondered why certain speakers say the same thing more than once in a speech? I have wondered that too. Perhaps it is because the audience as listeners are not listening well. Perhaps it is because what is being said is so important that it bears repeating.

Could it be Jesus wants us to capture an essential principle of following Him, which is to make the most of our time with what has been given to us? There are no entitlements in Jesus's backpack. He invites us to follow Him with no guarantees of a healthy life or a prosperous life as defined by the standards of the world.

The day my son died, my world was turned upside down and inside out. As I stated in my first book, *Reclaiming Heaven's Covenant: God's Blueprint to Restore All Relationships,* I lost my theology. My greatest concern was whether I would also lose my God. My theology was that in Jesus's backpack, there were certain guarantees in return for serving God—like healthy children. It turned out that was not in Jesus's backpack after all. Yet His invitation remained for me to follow Him. I chose to continue the journey with Jesus. He assured me I would see my son again if I would follow Him. I am banking on that promise!

Jesus teaches in this verse a truth about stewardship and obedience and work. If we apply ourselves, God will give us more responsibility. If we do not apply ourselves, God will use someone else.

Gospel Grit Challenge: Do you know what your spiritual gift is? How are you using it for God? Are you using your talents for God? Are you using your gifts for God?

T—LUKE 19:41: WHEN HE APPROACHED, HE SAW THE CITY AND WEPT OVER IT.

There are many places in this country where I would like to live. My top place would be New York City. (So if anyone reading this book could offer me a pastoring job there, my contact information is in the back.) As I proof this draft, I am seven days away from getting on a plane and spending seven days in the city that never sleeps! But there is nowhere in the world quite like the town we call home.

I live in a small town called Keizer, near Salem, the capital of Oregon. Keizer reminds me of Mayberry on *The Andy Griffith Show.* It is small enough that everything is familiar, and most of the time I run into somebody I know. I like that. We even have an annual parade.

Keizer is my Jerusalem. I have yet to find in my backpack tears for my city. That is because they are not in my backpack—they are in Jesus's. The truth is, Jesus weeps for all cities of the world because of His love for all people.

I have read biographies of famous preachers and evangelists who wept for the city they were to preach in. This teaching has made me ponder why I have no tears for Keizer. I would urge us to at least have tears for the cities we call home. Imagine the difference we could make if all the followers of Jesus Christ would find one soul to genuinely care about enough to share the love of Jesus with that person and invite him or her to join us in following Him!

Gospel Grit Challenge: Who could be your one in your city? Write that person's name down, start praying for him or her, and figure out how you can introduce this one to the man who wears the backpack!

S—LUKE 19:45: HE ENTERED THE TEMPLE AND BEGAN TO CAST OUT THOSE WHO WERE SELLING.

Today our church culture has turned the house of God into a coffeehouse, lounge, bar, restaurant, living room, game room, and probably some other things that will tick some of you off if I keep writing about them in this way. I understand we are all about reaching our culture. But this is a verse that could lead to some healthy and helpful conversation.

Jesus in this passage also said God's house was to be a house of prayer. How are we doing with this one? I know we have made lots of excuses in the name of reaching the lost. But is it possible we have made some compromises that have crossed over the line Jesus has drawn?

I know Jesus came to mix things up, but He also came to put some things back. Jesus appears to have a respect for the temple many of His followers do not have today. What would happen if we made the reading and teaching and preaching of the Word and prayer the main thing, the *only* thing in church? Have we turned church into a circus, a sideshow? Not all church events are such, but we must take a look at what we are producing and reproducing these days and ask if we are better off now than a generation ago. Have we turned singing in church into *American Idol* and elevated the band's performance to the level of a concert? Is it possible that with the very best of intentions, we have become a pathetic hybrid of what Jesus desires the church to be?

Is it possible that in our evolution of church, we have evolved so far away from the models in Scripture that we are hurting our cause and not helping it? Following Jesus means following the Bible. Having a biblical worldview means tying everything to the Bible. Is it possible we need to make some corrections based on this teaching from Jesus? I don't think most of us mean to do anything wrong. So will we follow Him into the temple and clean house? How much tradition do you have in your backpack? Jesus doesn't have any in His! How much personal preference do you have in your backpack? Jesus doesn't have any in His! All that counts for Him is the Father's will and the church He founded. Jesus's backpack is filled with relationships, first with His Father and then with us. The things we give Him from our backpack allow Him to help us more.

Gospel Grit Challenge: Evaluate the church you attend. Without having a critical spirit, ask yourself how much of what your church does can be supported by Scripture. Always try to bring about positive change in the church you are attending, bathed in prayer. Ultimately, if change does not occur and your spiritual growth or the growth of your family is being affected, life is too short and eternity too important to stay!

> T—LUKE 21:14: "SO MAKE UP YOUR MINDS NOT TO PREPARE BEFOREHAND TO DEFEND YOURSELVES."

One of the hardest things Jesus ever did was to remain silent before Pilate. Jesus could have done anything He wanted during that trial. Imagine the sights, the sounds, the smells of the hour. Jesus had completed his three-year hike. He had no money to pay for a lawyer. Unlike defendants in this country, He had no time to get cleaned up and put on nice clothes before He stood trial. Jesus must have looked pathetic before Pilate. No one could have imagined how much power He was holding back. Imagine being the Creator of the universe and just remaining silent before your creation.

Jesus is teaching us something profound here, which is to be prepared *not* to argue or defend ourselves, especially if we are right! This is tough to practice. Some days it just feels good to let someone have it. If anyone could have delivered a knockout blow, it would have been Jesus. Yet He kept silent.

How would our world be different if we argued less? I have a friend who has taught me a priceless message: make sure this is a hill worth dying on. That is exactly what Jesus did, but not the way we usually do it. He made sure by keeping quiet; His was a hill worth dying on.

Jesus is teaching us the importance of preparation. We are not to worry about what is planned for us; that is part of following Jesus. He takes care of the plans for our lives. But He does want us to be prepared for what comes our way. He is telling us not to be caught off guard or to be caught by surprise. We need to be ready and alert, as He taught in other passages. Put in your backpack the tool of silence, and give Jesus the tool of argumentation.

Gospel Grit Challenge: What things need to change in your life so you will be better prepared to take an insult without striking back?

T—LUKE 21:19: "BY YOUR ENDURANCE YOU WILL GAIN YOUR LIVES."

Following Jesus is about longevity. In our current culture, much of life is about getting it done fast. We want our food fast. We want our gas fast. We want our groceries fast. We want everything in life to come to us quickly. We want to get well fast. We want our schooling to go by fast. We are a product of our culture, in which technology is forcing us to speed up life. We want our news and information now. Waiting for something in this day and age is almost unacceptable.

Following Jesus goes against the grain of our culture. One reason Jesus wants us to follow Him is because He determines the length of the journey. Jesus does not take shortcuts anywhere! Jesus never cuts corners. Jesus is all about relationships, and relationships take time.

I love to buy and sell things, especially things that are considered collectibles. I did it long before the reality shows on television where they find something for nothing and sell it for something. Had I only known reality TV was coming, I could have been the host of one of those shows. I have found some interesting things along the way over the years of picking.

One thing I have noticed about items made before 1965 or so is that the quality is better than it is now. I also notice that everything was made in the USA. Just about everything we buy today is junk and is made in China. What is wrong with us? Why have we become so cheap and lazy? I love the items I find because their quality is brilliant.

Following Jesus takes time because great relationships take time and doing anything with excellence takes time. Following Jesus is about following Him all the way! Following Jesus is about the campfire. Following Jesus is about stopping once in a while, emptying out the backpack, and talking about what we have collected along the trail. Following Jesus is all about endurance. There is a prize waiting for those who will follow Him to the end!

Gospel Grit Challenge: Identify what causes you to lose focus on Jesus. Identify ways you can build up your endurance as you follow Him. Be specific!

T—LUKE 21:28: "BUT WHEN THESE THINGS BEGIN TO TAKE PLACE, STRAIGHTEN UP AND LIFT UP YOUR HEADS, BECAUSE YOUR REDEMPTION IS DRAWING NEAR."

Jesus wants the end to come more than we do. I was never too concerned about the end of the world as we know it until my son went home to be with the Lord. Then I wanted the end to come immediately. Jesus gives us warning signs along the way so we can recognize when the end is near.

Perhaps the condition and events of the world today are a sign the end is near. Perhaps genocide and all the desperate people in the world are signs the end is near. Perhaps world hunger is a sign the end is near. Perhaps the signs are so big we are ignoring the obvious.

Followers of Jesus have always thought Jesus was coming back in their generation, all the way back to the first-century disciples. Those who follow closely to Him want His return to happen sooner than later. Every generation hopes it will be their generation that never tastes of death. I am not one of those who predict future events or go up on a mountain to wait for the world to implode. However, I honestly believe we are living in the last days and the end is near.

I am writing books and preaching with a sense of urgency, and I feel within my spirit that Jesus is about to make His presence known to the world with His mighty return. I am not going to sell my home and become homeless, nor am I going to quit my job and become unemployed thinking the end is days away. But I do have my backpack packed, and I am totally ready for Jesus to come get me. As soon as I can, I am going to turn it in for the keys to my mansion and eternal life! I urge you to follow Jesus closely all the way to the end of the finish line!

Gospel Grit Challenge: Identify the prophecies in Scripture that still need fulfilling before Jesus can return. Name the prophecies that have been fulfilled in the last one hundred years. These are exciting times we live in!

S—LUKE 22:39: HE CAME OUT AND PROCEEDED AS WAS HIS CUSTOM TO THE MOUNT OF OLIVES.

Jesus had some routine in His unusual life of ministry, and He had some favorite little spots He enjoyed. I sometimes wonder whether when He created the earth, He created special places knowing He would walk in those very places.

When we are under pressure, routine is good. When we are under a lot of stress, having a safe place to go is a good thing. Having a special place to get away where we love the surroundings is healthy. We are told Jesus went to the Mount of Olives on a regular basis. Remember, we are following Him, so we are going to the Mount of Olives with Jesus. Jesus needs to get away, and so do we. Some people take advantage of this privilege; most do not.

I would imagine that while at the Mount of Olives, Jesus sat in a favorite location and there took off that infamous backpack. I imagine He might even have emptied it out to make sure He had collected everything He needed before going to the cross. Remember, He eventually exchanged the backpack for a cross. Not a great deal for Jesus, but a great deal for us!

Try to picture Jesus going through all the items in His backpack one at a time. As you are observing, Jesus pulls out something of yours. You recognize it. You don't want to recognize it. You realize it was a dark day in your life, and Jesus rolled your burden onto Him. You are now able to put following Jesus into sharp focus. These are the times the Holy Spirit shows us clearly how involved Jesus is in our daily lives. You realize like never before that as you have followed Him, He has done more for you than you remember. He rarely empties the backpack. On this special occasion, He empties it not to show off, but to show you how much He loves you.

Gospel Grit Challenge: Identify the dark days you have given Jesus throughout your lifetime and the burdens He has taken from you so you could live a happy life. I invite you to bow your head and tell Jesus thank you!

S—LUKE 24:25: THEN HE OPENED THEIR MINDS TO UNDERSTAND THE SCRIPTURES.

I have sometimes wondered why Jesus does not do this all of the time for all of us. I would think He would want us to understand the

Scriptures every time we read them. Often, however, He *does* do it. When you read your Bible, do you invite the Holy Spirit to reveal to you truth? If not, give it a try.

I have been a Christian for over forty-five years, and the Bible is fresh every time I read it. I love when I learn something brand-new for the first time. I love sharing my new insight with my wife, my congregation, anybody who will listen.

Imagine the perspective we will have on the Scriptures when we get to heaven. Imagine the lessons we will learn from Scripture as Jesus is teaching it to us! Perspective is everything. I trust that thinking about the Gospels from a perspective of backpacks, homelessness, and unemployment has helped you better understand the teaching of Jesus. We have but one more book to explore, and then our three years with Jesus will be completed. The great news is we will still be following Him. Actually, our three years with Him are a crash course on how to make it out alive from this life and get to heaven too!

The picture I hope you have captured in these pages is that just as Jesus needed no home or job, neither did He really need a backpack. He shouldered it only so we could better understand what it means to follow Him!

Gospel Grit Challenge: Identify some of the new truths you have learned from the Gospels from the perspective of a God who is hiking through Israel unemployed and homeless. Be specific!

SCRIPTURES FROM LUKE
FOR FURTHER STUDY

380. S—Luke 2:46: When He was about twelve years old, His parents found Him in the temple, sitting in the midst of the teachers, both listening to them and asking them questions.

381. T—Luke 2:49: "Did you not know that I had to be in My Father's house?"

382. S—Luke 2:51: He continued in subjection to His parents.

383. S—Luke 2:52: Jesus kept increasing in wisdom and stature, and in favor with God and men.

384. T—Luke 3:21–23: Jesus was also baptized, and while He was praying, Heaven was opened, and the Holy Spirit descended upon Him in bodily form like a dove, and a voice came out of Heaven, "You are My beloved Son, in You I am well-pleased."

385. S—Luke 3:23: Jesus was about thirty years of age when He began His ministry.

386. S—Luke 4:1–2: Jesus, full of the Holy Spirit, returned from the Jordan and was led about by the Spirit in the wilderness for forty days; and when those days had ended, He became hungry.

387. T—Luke 4:4: "It is written, 'Man shall not live on bread alone.'"

388. T—Luke 4:8: "It is written, 'You shall worship the Lord your God and serve Him only.'"

389. T—Luke 4:12: "It is said, 'You shall not put the Lord your God to the test.'"

390. S—Luke 4:14: Jesus returned to Galilee in the power of the Spirit.

391. S—Luke 4:15: He began teaching in their synagogues and was praised by all.

392. S—Luke 4:16: As was His custom, He entered the synagogue on the Sabbath, and stood up to read.

393. T—Luke 4:18–19: "The Spirit of the Lord is upon Me, because He anointed Me to preach the gospel to the poor. He has sent Me to

proclaim release to the captives, and recovery of sight to the blind, to set free those who are oppressed, to proclaim the favorable year of the Lord."

394. S—Luke 4:20: He closed the book, gave it back to the attendant, and sat down.

395. T—Luke 4:24: "No prophet is welcome in his hometown."

396. S—Luke 4:30: But passing through their midst, He went His way.

397. S—Luke 4:31: He was teaching them on the Sabbath.

398. T—Luke 4:35: Jesus rebuked him, saying, "Be quiet and come out of him!"

399. S—Luke 4:39: Standing over Simon's mother-in-law, He rebuked the fever, and it left her.

400. S—Luke 4:40–41: Laying His hands on every one of them, He healed them. And demons also came out of many.

401. S—Luke 4:42: When day came, He departed and went to a lonely place.

402. T—Luke 4:43: "I must preach the kingdom of God to the other cities also, for I was sent for this purpose."

403. S—Luke 4:44: He kept on preaching in the synagogues of Judea.

404. S—Luke 5:3: He sat down and began teaching the people from the boat.

405. T—Luke 5:10: "Do not fear, from now on you will be catching men."

406. T—Luke 5:13: He stretched out His hand and touched Him saying, "I am willing; be cleansed." And immediately the leprosy left Him.

407. S—Luke 5:15: Great crowds gathered to hear Him and to be healed of their sicknesses.

408. S—Luke 5:16: But He Himself would often slip away to the wilderness to pray.

409. S—Luke 5:17: And it came about one day that He was teaching.

410. S—Luke 5:20: And seeing their faith . . .

411. T—Luke 5:24: "But so that you may know that the Son of Man has authority on earth to forgive sins,"—He said to the paralytic—

"I say to you get up, and pick up your stretcher and go home."

412. T—Luke 5:27: To Levi the tax collector: "Follow Me."

413. T—Luke 5:32: "I have not come to call the righteous but sinners to repentance."

414. S—Luke 5:36: He told them a parable.

415. S—Luke 6:6: On another Sabbath, He entered the synagogue and taught.

416. S—Luke 6:10: Jesus healed a withered hand on the Sabbath.

417. S—Luke 6:12: He went off to the mountain to pray, and He spent the whole night in prayer to God.

418. S—Luke 6:13: He called His disciples to Him and chose twelve of them.

419. S—Luke 6:19: All the people were trying to touch Him, for power was coming from Him and healing them all.

420. T—Luke 6:27–31: "But I say to you who hear, love your enemies, do good to those who hate you, bless those who curse you, pray for those who mistreat you. Whoever hits you on the cheek, offer him the other also; and whoever takes away your coat, do not withhold your shirt from him either. Give to everyone who asks of you, and whoever takes away what is yours, do not demand it back. Treat others the same way you want them to treat you."

421. T—Luke 6:35: "But love your enemies, and do good, and lend, expecting nothing in return."

422. T—Luke 6:36: "Be merciful, just as your Father is merciful."

423. T—Luke 6:37: "And do not judge, and you will not be judged; and do not condemn, and you will not be condemned; pardon, and you will be pardoned."

424. T—Luke 6:38: "Give, and it will be given to you. They will pour into your lap good measure—pressed down, shaken together, and running over. For by your standard of measure, it will be measured to you in return."

425. S—Luke 6:39: He also spoke a parable to them.

426. T—Luke 6:41: "Why do you look at the speck that is in your brother's eye, but you do not notice the log that is in your own eye?"

427. T—Luke 6:47–49: "Everyone who comes to Me, and hears My words and acts on them, I will show you whom he is like: he is like a man building a house, who dug deep and laid a foundation on the rock; and when a flood occurred, the torrent burst against that house and could not shake it, because it had been well built. But the one who has heard, and has not acted accordingly, is like a man who built a house upon the ground without any foundation; and the torrent burst against it and immediately it collapsed, and the ruin of that house was great."

428. S—Luke 7:1: He completed all His discourse in the hearing of the people.

429. T—Luke 7:9: "I say to you, not even in Israel have I found such a great faith."

430. S—Luke 7:13: He felt compassion for her.

431. S—Luke 7:15: The dead man sat up and began to speak.

432. S—Luke 7:21: He cured many people of diseases and afflictions and evil spirits, and He gave sight to many who were blind.

433. T—Luke 7:23: "Blessed is he who does not take offense at Me."

434. S—Luke 7:36: He entered the Pharisee's house and reclined at the table to eat.

435. T—Luke 7:47: "For this reason I say to you, her sins, which are many, have been forgiven, for she loved much; but he who is forgiven little, loves little."

436. S—Luke 8:1: He began going around from one city and village to another, proclaiming and preaching the kingdom of God; and the twelve were with Him.

437. S—Luke 8:4: He spoke by way of a parable.

438. T—Luke 8:18: "So take care how you listen; for whoever has, to him more shall be given; and whoever does not have, even what he thinks he has shall be taken away from him."

439. T—Luke 8:21: "My mother and My brothers are these who hear the word of God and do it."

440. S—Luke 8:23: But as they were sailing along, He fell asleep.

441. S—Luke 8:24: When the disciples woke Jesus, He rebuked the

wind and the surging waves, and they stopped, and it became calm.

442. S—Luke 8:33: The demons [Legion] came out from the man and entered the swine.

443. T—Luke 8:39: To the man from whom the demons came out: "Return to your house and describe what great things God has done for you."

444. T—Luke 8:48: To the woman who touched Jesus in the crowd: "Daughter, your faith has made you well; go in peace."

445. T—Luke 8:50: "Do not be afraid any longer; only believe, and she will be made well."

446. S—Luke 8:55: Jesus brought Jairus's twelve-year-old daughter back to life. (Jairus was an official of the synagogue.) When her spirit returned, she got up immediately and Jesus gave orders for something to be given to her to eat.

447. S—Luke 9:1–2: He called the twelve together and gave them power and authority over all the demons, and to heal all diseases. He sent them out to proclaim the kingdom of God, and to heal diseases.

448. S—Luke 9:10: Taking the disciples with Him, He went to a city called Bethsaida.

449. S—Luke 9:11: Welcoming the crowds, He spoke to them about the kingdom of God and cured those who had need of healing.

450. S—Luke 9:16: He took the five loaves and two fish, and looking up to heaven, He blessed them, and broke them, and kept giving them to the disciples to set before the people.

451. S—Luke 9:18: He was praying alone.

452. T—Luke 9:23: "If anyone wishes to come after Me, he must deny himself, and take up his cross daily and follow Me."

453. T—Luke 9:24: "For whoever wishes to save his life will lose it, but whoever loses his life for My sake, he is the one who will save it."

454. T—Luke 9:26: "For whoever is ashamed of Me and My words, the Son of Man will be ashamed of him when He comes in His glory, and the glory of the father and of the holy angels."

455. S—Luke 9:28: He took Peter, John, and James up to the mountain to pray.

456. S—Luke 9:42: Jesus knew what they were thinking in their hearts.

457. T—Luke 9:48: "Whoever receives this child in My name receives Me, and whoever receives Me receives Him who sent Me; for the one who is least among you, this is the one who is great."

458. T—Luke 9:56: "For the Son of Man did not come to destroy men's lives, but to save them."

459. T—Luke 9:59: "Follow Me."

460. T—Luke 9:60: "Allow the dead to bury their own dead; but as for you, go and proclaim everywhere the kingdom of God."

461. S—Luke 10:1: The Lord appointed seventy others and sent them in pairs ahead of Him to every city and place where He Himself was going to come.

462. T—Luke 10:2: "Therefore beseech the Lord of the harvest to send out laborers into His harvest."

463. T—Luke 10:19–20: "Behold, I have given you authority to tread on serpents and scorpions, and over all the power of the enemy, and nothing will injure you. Nevertheless do not rejoice in this, that the spirits are subject to you, but rejoice that your names are recorded in Heaven."

464. S—Luke 10:21: At that very time, He rejoiced greatly in the Holy Spirit.

465. T—Luke 10:37: "To conclude the parable of the Good Samaritan: Go and do the same."

466. S—Luke 11:1: While He was praying, His disciples asked Him to teach them to pray.

467. T—Luke 11:2–4: "When you pray, say: 'Father, hallowed be Your name. Your kingdom come. Give us each day our daily bread. And forgive us our sins, for we ourselves also forgive everyone who is indebted to us. And lead us not into temptation.'"

468. T—Luke 11:9: "Ask, and it will be given to you; seek, and you will find; knock, and it will be opened to you."

469. S—Luke 11:14: He cast out a demon who had made a man mute.

470. S—Luke 11:17: He knew their thoughts.

471. T—Luke 11:23: "He who is not with Me is against Me; and he who does not gather with Me, scatters."

472. T—Luke 11:28: "On the contrary, blessed are those who hear the word of God and observe it." (Speaking against blessing Mary, His mother.)

473. T—Luke 11:35: "Then watch out that the light in you is not darkness."

474. T—Luke 11:41: "But give that which is within as charity, and then all things are clean for you."

475. T—Luke 11:39–52: Woes upon the Pharisees.

476. T—Luke 12:1: "Beware of the leaven of the Pharisees, which is hypocrisy."

477. T—Luke 12:4: "My friends, do not be afraid of those who kill the body and after that have no more that they can do."

478. T—Luke 12:5: "But I will warn you whom to fear: fear the One who, after He has killed, has authority to cast into hell; yes, I tell you, fear Him!"

479. T—Luke 12:7: "Do not fear."

480. T—Luke 12:8–10. "Everyone who confesses Me before men, the Son of Man will confess him also before the angels of God; but he who denies Me before men will be denied before the angels of God. And everyone who speaks a word against the Son of Man, it will not be forgiven him."

481. T—Luke 12:11–12: "Do not worry about how or what you are to speak in your defense, or what you are to say; for the Holy Spirit will teach you in that very hour what you ought to say."

482. T—Luke 12:15: "Beware, and be on your guard against every form of greed."

483. S—Luke 12:16: He told them a parable.

484. T—Luke 12:21: "So is the man who lays up treasure for himself, and is not rich toward God."

485. T—Luke 12:22: "Do not worry about your life, as to what you will eat; nor for your body, as to what you will put on."

486. T—Luke 12:24: "Consider the ravens."

487. T—Luke 12:27: "Consider the lilies."

488. T—Luke 12:29: "Do not seek what you will eat and what you will drink, and do not keep worrying."

489. T—Luke 12:31: "But seek His kingdom."

490. T—Luke 12:32: "Do not be afraid."

491. T—Luke 12:33: "Sell your possessions and give to charity."

492. T—Luke 12:35: "Be dressed in readiness, and keep your lamps lit."

493. T—Luke 12:40: Regarding the return of Jesus: "You too, be ready."

494. T—Luke 13:3: "Unless you repent, you will all likewise perish."

495. T—Luke 13:5: "Unless you repent, you will all likewise perish."

496. S—Luke 13:6: He began telling a parable.

497. S—Luke 13:10: He taught in one of the synagogues on the Sabbath.

498. S—Luke 13:11–12: Jesus healed a woman who had been sick for eighteen years with a spirit.

499 S—Luke 13:13: He laid His hands on her.

500. S—Luke 13:22: He passed through from one city and village to another, teaching and proceeding on His way to Jerusalem.

501. T—Luke 13:24: "Strive to enter through the narrow door; for many, I tell you, will seek to enter and will not be able."

502. S—Luke 14:1: He went into a Pharisee's house on the Sabbath to eat.

503. S—Luke 14:4: Jesus healed a man with dropsy.

504. S—Luke 14:7: He began to speak a parable to the invited guests.

505. T—Luke 14:11: "For everyone who exalts himself will be humbled, and he who humbles himself will be exalted."

506. T—Luke 14:13: "When you give a reception, invite the poor, the crippled, the lame, the blind."

507. T—Luke 14:26–27: "If anyone comes to Me, and does not hate his own father and mother and wife and children and brothers and sisters, yes, and even his own life, he cannot by My disciple. Whoever does not carry his own cross and come after Me cannot be My disciple."

508. T—Luke 14:33: "So then, none of you can be My disciple who does not give up all his own possessions."

509. S—Luke 15:3: He told them a parable.

510. T—Luke 15:7: "I tell you in the same way, there will be more joy in heaven over one sinner who repents than over ninety-nine righteous persons who need no repentance."

511. T—Luke 15:10: "In the same way, I tell you, there is more joy in the presence of the angels of God over one sinner who repents."

512. T—Luke 16:9: "Make friends for yourselves by means of the wealth of unrighteousness, so that when it fails, they will receive you into eternal dwellings."

513. T—Luke 16:10: "He who is faithful in a very little thing is faithful also in much; and he who is unrighteous in a very little thing is unrighteous also in much."

514. T—Luke 16:13: "No servant can serve two masters...You cannot serve God and wealth."

515. T—Luke 16:18: "Everyone who divorces his wife and marries another commits adultery, and he who marries one who is divorced from a husband commits adultery."

516. T—Luke 17:3–4: "Be on your guard! If your brother sins, rebuke him; and if he repents, forgive him. And if he sins against you seven times a day, and returns to you seven times, saying 'I repent,' forgive him."

517. T—Luke 17:6: "If you had faith like a mustard seed, you would say to this mulberry tree, 'Be uprooted and be planted in the sea'; and it would obey you."

518. T—Luke 17:14: "Go and show yourselves to the priest." (The healing of the ten lepers.)

519. T—Luke 17:17–18: "Were there not ten cleansed? But the nine—where are they? Was no one found who returned to give glory to God, except this foreigner?"

520. T—Luke 17:19: "Stand up and go; your faith has made you well."

521. T—Luke 17:32: "Remember Lot's wife."

522. T—Luke 17:33: "Whoever seeks to keep his life will lose it, and

whoever loses his life will preserve it."

523. S—Luke 18:1: He told them a parable to show that at all times they ought to pray and not to lose heart.

524. S—Luke 18:9: He also told this parable to certain ones who trusted in themselves that they were righteous and viewed others with contempt.

525. T—Luke 18:16–17: "Permit the children to come to Me, and do not hinder them, for the kingdom of God belongs to such as these. Truly I say to you, whoever does not receive the kingdom of God like a child will not enter it at all."

526. T—Luke 18:22: "One thing you still lack; sell all that you possess and distribute it to the poor, and you shall have treasure in heaven; and come, follow Me."

527. T—Luke 18:24: "How hard it is for those who are wealthy to enter the kingdom of God!"

528. T—Luke 18:27: "The things that are impossible with people are possible with God."

529. S—Luke 18:31: He took the twelve aside and spoke to them.

530. T—Luke 18:42: "Receive your sight; your faith has made you well."

531. T—Luke 19:5: "Zacchaeus, hurry and come down, for today I must stay at your house."

532. T—Luke 19:10: "For the Son of Man has come to seek and to save that which was lost."

533. S—Luke 19:11: He went on to tell them a parable.

534. T—Luke 19:26: "I tell you that to everyone who has, more shall be given, but from the one who does not have, even what he does have shall be taken away."

535. S—Luke 19:41: When He approached, He saw the city and wept over it.

536. S—Luke 19:45: He entered the temple and began to cast out those who were selling.

537. T—Luke 19:46: "My house shall be a house of prayer, but you have made it a robbers' den."

538. S—Luke 19:47: He taught daily in the temple.

539. S—Luke 20:1: While He was teaching the people in the temple area and preaching the gospel, the religious leaders confronted Him.

540. S—Luke 20:9: He began to tell the people a parable.

541. S—Luke 20:23: He detected their trickery.

542. T—Luke 20:25: "Then render to Caesar the things that are Caesar's, and to God the things that are God's."

543. T—Luke 20:46–47: "Beware of the scribes, who like to walk around in long robes, and love respectful greetings in the market places, and chief seats in the synagogues and places of honor at banquets, who devour widows' houses, and for appearance's sake offer long prayers. These will receive greater condemnation."

544. S—Luke 21:1: He looked up and saw the rich putting their gifts into the treasury.

545. S—Luke 21:2: He saw a poor widow putting in two small copper coins.

546. T—Luke 21:8: "See to it that you are not misled."

547. T—Luke 21:9: "When you hear of wars and rumors and disturbances, do not be terrified."

548. T—Luke 21:14: "So make up your minds not to prepare beforehand to defend yourselves."

549. T—Luke 21:19: "By your endurance you will gain your lives."

550. T—Luke 21:28: "But when these things begin to take place, straighten up and lift up your heads, because your redemption is drawing near."

551. S—Luke 21:29: He told them a parable.

552. T—Luke 21:31: "So you also, when you see things happening, recognize that the kingdom of God is near."

553. T—Luke 21:34: "Be on guard, that your hearts may not be weighted down with dissipation and drunkenness and the worries of life."

554. T—Luke 21:36: "But keep on the alert at all times, praying that you may have strength to escape all these things that are about to

take place, and to stand before the Son of Man."

555. S—Luke 21:37: During the day He taught in the temple, but at evening he went out and spent the night on the mount that is called Olivet.

556. S—Luke 22:17: He took the cup and gave thanks.

557. T—Luke 22:19: When He had taken some bread and given thanks, He broke it and gave it to them, saying, "This is My body which is given for you; do this in remembrance of Me."

558. T—Luke 22:26: "The one who is the greatest among you must become like the youngest, and the leader like the servant."

559. T—Luke 22:32: "But I have prayed for you, that your faith may not fail; and you, when once you have turned again, strengthen your brothers."

560. S—Luke 22:39: He came out and proceeded as was His custom to the Mount of Olives.

561. T—Luke 22:40: "Pray that you may not enter into temptation."

562. S—Luke 22:41: He withdrew from them about a stone's throw, and He knelt down and began to pray.

563. T—Luke 22:42: "Father, if You are willing, remove this cup from Me; yet not My will, but Yours be done."

564. S—Luke 22:44: In agony, He prayed very fervently, and His sweat became like drops of blood.

565. T—Luke 22:46: "Get up and pray that you may not enter into temptation."

566. T—Luke 22:51: As He healed the ear of the guard: "Stop! No more of this."

567. S—Luke 23:9: Pilate questioned Jesus at some length, but He answered him nothing.

568. T—Luke 23:34: "Father, forgive them; for they do not know what they are doing."

569. T—Luke 23:43: "Truly I say to you, today you shall be with Me in Paradise."

570. S—Luke 23:46: Jesus cried out with a loud voice.

571. T—Luke 24:25: "O foolish men and slow of heart to believe in all

that the prophets have spoken."

572. S—Luke 24:27: He explained to them the things concerning Himself in all the Scriptures.

573. S—Luke 24:30: He took the bread and blessed it, and breaking it, He began giving it to them.

574. T—Luke 24:38: "Why are you troubled, and why do doubts arise in your hearts?"

575. S—Luke 24:40: He showed them His hands and His feet.

576. S—Luke 24:42–43: He took a piece of broiled fish and ate it before them.

577. S—Luke 24:25: Then He opened their minds to understand the Scriptures.

578. T—Luke 24:47: "And that repentance for forgiveness of sins would be proclaimed in His name to all the nations, beginning from Jerusalem."

579. T—Luke 24:49: "But you are to stay in the city until you are clothed with power from on high."

580. S—Luke 24:50: He led them out as far as Bethany, and He lifted up His hands and blessed them.

GOSPEL GRIT
John

As I indicated I would in some of my earlier writings in this book, I recently went elk hunting in the mountains of the Oregon coast. The scenery is breathtaking. Roosevelt elk are even more breathtaking when seen in the wild. I have a friend who has been hunting these mountains for twenty-eight years, and he is an awesome hunter. He is a tough, rugged, almost animal-like man in the woods. His skills are greater than any I have ever seen out there. He scales the mountains like a cougar. He wades through creeks, rivers, and swamps like an alligator. For two days I followed his every step looking for the elusive elk.

On my back, I carried a backpack filled with everything needed for survival in case I got lost or had to spend the night in the woods. I noticed my friend had a backpack too, but it was smaller and lighter than mine. As we journeyed through the virgin jungle of the Oregon Coastal Mountains, I began to realize the parallels between my time with my friend and my time backpacking with Jesus.

Life does not always turn out like we plan it. Before our hunting trip ended, I contracted a severe case of poison oak somewhere along the way and ended up in urgent care when I got home and medicated with steroids for two weeks. Such is the life of a hunter. Did I get an elk? No. Did I get a bad case of poison oak? Yes.

There's a lesson to be learned here. Backpacking with Jesus, like hunting in the mountains, is not about fairy tales and birthday parties and tropical islands. Backpacking with Jesus takes grit—gospel grit!

John, like Matthew, was one of Jesus's original twelve disciples. He recorded His experiences backpacking with Jesus in his Gospel. He seemed to notice different things than Matthew did, so many of the challenges Jesus gives in the Gospel of John are unique to that book.

Let's get back on the road with Jesus!

S—JOHN 1:14: AND THE WORD BECAME FLESH, AND DWELT AMONG US, AND WE SAW HIS GLORY, GLORY AS OF THE ONLY BEGOTTEN FROM THE FATHER, FULL OF GRACE AND TRUTH.

This verse is the bottom line of redemption. Jesus came to fix what we broke. We broke God's plan and purpose for us so badly there was no way on earth we could fix it. There were not enough animals on Planet Earth to sacrifice to remedy our illness. So God did what He knew He would do from day one: He stepped in and created a cure for our illness in the laboratories of heaven. His cure was His Son, Jesus Christ!

Not only did Jesus pay the price for our sin, but He also built a bridge for us to cross over so we could reach God again. Jesus restored what was lost in the garden of Eden: the potential to once again walk with God!

While out hunting with my friend, one of the last hurdles we had to cross before coming out of the woods on the second day was a swamp. The very last section of this swamp included a deep channel we had to wade through. I did not want to go through that swamp. But in order to get out of the woods and get home to the doctor, I had no alternative.

My friend went first as I watched him wade through muddy, murky water over his waist. He stood on the other side and said to come on over. I stood there just looking at him, praying there was another way. But I knew better. There was no other way to get home. I had to grit my teeth and go for it. As I got to the other side, he was there waiting for me with a big grin.

Jesus has already crossed the swamps of life on our behalf. He asks us to carry our cross and come over to join Him. The swamps look overwhelming some days. Life can be dark and murky and muddy. We must remember that Jesus has already crossed over onto dry land and is waiting for us to follow Him. When we reach the other side, I am certain He will meet us with a grin bigger than my friend's grin. Following Jesus includes the cross.

Gospel Grit Challenge: What obstacle is staring you in the face today that you are avoiding? What do you need to cross over to meet Jesus, who has already walked the waters He asks you to walk through? Sometimes we need to have faith like a child and jump in the water without giving it any more thought!

T—JOHN 2:16: "TAKE THESE THINGS AWAY; STOP MAKING MY FATHER'S HOUSE A PLACE OF BUSINESS."

The church is a business. How in the world are we going to get away from this fact? I spend more time administrating my church than I do preparing for messages or praying. I believe Jesus is talking here about priorities and focus. Our priority needs to be to worship God and keep our focus on Jesus Christ. We can easily get sidetracked in this life. Jesus is asking His followers to stay focused.

When walking through the woods that dreadful day with my friend, I failed to watch where he had just stepped. I missed a log and fell down a hill into the stickers about eight feet down. It was miserable and painful and unnecessary. Why had I missed it? I was busy looking at something out of the corner of my eye. In the process I took my eye off the one I was following and made a dangerous misstep.

Jesus is telling us to keep our focus on Him or we may find ourselves in the stickers of life. Following Jesus is a 24/7 proposition. He tells us to follow Him each step of the way because we never know when the next step will be a hole in the ground—or a land mine.

In church life, following Jesus is especially necessary because getting sidetracked seems to be the norm. We end up down trails God never intended the church to go down. God wants us to stay on the trail Jesus has blazed. When we stay on His trail we will follow in His footsteps, and we will do the right things in church, not the wrong things.

Gospel Grit Challenge: Evaluate your participation in your church. Have you made it a house of worship? Have you made it a house of prayer? Do you go to get fed and to feed others, or has it become something else for you? How can you fix your church life by fixing your eyes on Jesus?

S—JOHN 2:24: FOR HIS PART, JESUS DID NOT ENTRUST HIMSELF TO THEM, FOR HE KNEW ALL MEN.

We have a fair number of homeless people in our town. At first glance, it would be easy to think they either are lazy or do not know very much, or to think something else that is derogatory and probably totally false. At first glance, Jesus did not get a lot of respect from the religious elite. They thought He was some sort of a strange duck. They wrote Him off as a lunatic. One small factor they failed to understand: Jesus was the Son of God!

People at times are misleading. I was always taught to have good gear when you hunt. A hunter is only as good as the gear he wears, or so I thought. My friend wears a pathetic pair of tennis shoes when hunting in the woods. My first time out with him, I wore a pair of boots made for hunting. It turned out I was wrong. I ended up with blisters the size of a silver dollar, one on each heel, while my friend trotted through the woods with the greatest of ease. After all, you do not go through swamps with boots. You go through swamps with the lightest shoe possible so your foot can dry out! I have learned much from my hunting partner. I have learned not to worry so much about looks when I should worry about being practical.

Jesus is completely practical when He tells us to follow Him. He may look like your typical homeless unemployed backpacker, but He is not. Jesus is the Son of God!

Gospel Grit Challenge: How much do you worry about how you look?
Are there ways you can be more concerned about being practical as
a follower of Jesus Christ than about your appearance to others? Who
are you trying to impress more, man or Jesus?

T—JOHN 4:24: "GOD IS SPIRIT, AND THOSE WHO WORSHIP HIM MUST
WORSHIP IN SPIRIT AND TRUTH."

Jesus's coming to earth is what makes God real in our lives. Jesus tells us His Father is spirit. The problem we have with spirit is that we never see it. We are made of flesh and bones, and we need to see God. That's why Jesus came. Even at that, those of us living today still have not seen Him in the flesh, although someday we will. This is what makes the earthly life of Jesus so special. I don't care that He was homeless and unemployed; He was real!

After hours of hiking up steep mountains in terrain fit only for animals, I stopped to rest my weary bones out on the trail. I took off my backpack and rested beside a quiet stream of water. I did not realize how heavy my pack had become until I took it off. We experience the same thing in life. We forget how much of a load we carry until we actually give it to God and let Him take it for us.

It was on this little rest that my friend asked me why I had so much in my pack. I told him I thought I needed all those things to survive. He simply smiled and said, "As long as you are with me, you do not need all those things." Wow! I instantly thought of backpacking with Jesus and realizing that is exactly what He says to us.

We fill our packs with material things to survive and fail to recognize how real God is. Our inability to see Him and touch Him and talk with Him in person creates an anxiety that makes us want to fill up our backpacks just to survive. Jesus allows time to rest on the trail. Perhaps today He is calling for you to take the load off your back and realize that though spirit, He is very real, and the things "needed" for survival may not be needed after all!

The reality is that the Spirit of God is more real than what you have in your backpack. When you get tired in life, you need to stop to rest, remove your pack, and realize God is greater than the "securities" you are carrying.

Gospel Grit Challenge: Write down the things in your life that worry you. Now, release those to God and take time today, right now, to worship Him in spirit and in truth. Allow God to become real in your life through Jesus Christ.

S—JOHN 4:41: MANY MORE BELIEVED BECAUSE OF WHAT JESUS SAID.

Honestly, sometimes it is hard to believe the things Jesus says because they require faith on our part. Jesus spoke to many people during His three years of homelessness. Some followed Him, and some did not.

Taking Jesus at His word, especially when it is foreign to us, can be hard. Yet, it is a part of following Jesus. I grew up with a saying, and I have stuck with it as an adult: "God said it, I believe it, and that settles it."

If you are a Christian, do not doubt what Jesus says; follow what Jesus says. You will never regret obeying Jesus. It always pays off!

My hunting partner assured me we would see elk. When carrying a bow and arrow through the woods looking for a mammoth of an animal, it does not seem possible to actually see one. I have been let down many times before by experts in the field, so when my friend said we would see elk, I began to rewind those empty prophecies in my head from trips from the past.

The first afternoon we were hunting, we were hiking what seemed to be miles away from our targeted area. My friend told me it had everything to do with the direction of the wind. If the critter picked up our scent, we would never see it again. We went, according to my friend, five or six miles out of our way to have the wind in our favor. Every step I took was a step of doubt. It seemed as if we were always going in the wrong direction.

At 5:45 after hunting all day, I heard a loud crunch just ahead of me in the river. I ran up to a log that stood up to my chest on the ground, peered over, and saw a beautiful Roosevelt elk. I didn't get a shot off, but that was not my goal. My goal was to see elk, and elk I saw.

It turned out my friend knew exactly what he was doing. Sometimes if we want to see something special in this life, we may have to go out of our way to find it. Jesus may be taking you down a road that seems far from where you want to be. He does this because He knows that in the proper time, if we do things His way, we will see things that can only be provided for by God. If you are spinning your wheels in life and feel frustrated, as long as you are following Jesus, you can know that He is setting you up to see something very special. For this, I thank my friend for the detour. Without it I would never have seen that beautiful elk!

Gospel Grit Challenge: Name the detours God has taken you on. Identify your most recent detour. We either follow Jesus and expect what He says will be true, or we do it our way and never see anything special in life!

T—JOHN 5:14: "DO NOT SIN ANYMORE, SO THAT NOTHING WORSE HAPPENS TO YOU."

Sin has consequences. I spoke with a young woman today who was feeling guilt from her past. She was having a hard time accepting the love and forgiveness Jesus offered her. She had a backpack with her past in it. I told her she had weights in there God hadn't put there. I explained to her that while she was unaware, the enemy had put doubt and guilt in her backpack. What a tremendous truth it is to know we are forgiven! There are some things that do not belong in our backpack. Sin does not belong in our backpack. Guilt does not belong in our backpack.

Sin can be compared to a bottle of poison. If the bottle is clearly marked, then we know not to mess with what is in there. But if we were to remove the label and put something unassuming on it, we make what is inside the bottle more dangerous, not less dangerous. This is the nature of sin. We live in a culture that wants to call sin everything *but* sin. We make the poison more dangerous by deceiving ourselves. We have not diluted what is inside the bottle at all! Jesus is teaching us along our way in life to be honest about sin and call it for what it is. How we approach sin definitely affects our quality of life.

> *Gospel Grit Challenge: Are there areas in your life where you have compromised with sin? Identify them and redefine them for the dangerous things they actually are. If you have asked forgiveness, then leave it with Jesus and know you are forgiven. If you are dealing with guilt, trust Jesus to release you from the thoughts you are struggling with and ask God for His peace that goes beyond all human understanding that He may guard your heart and mind in Christ Jesus.*

S—JOHN 6:6: HE TESTED PHILIP; HE KNEW WHAT HE INTENDED TO DO.

The cool thing about following Jesus is that He knows when we are going to follow Him and when we are not going to follow Him. He may have His back to us, but He always keeps track of our every step.

When I was in the woods with my friend, he rarely would look back. He just kept going and expected me to keep going. He knew he was faster and stronger than me and that I could never keep up with him, yet he kept going. On one stretch where it was very steep, he looked back long enough to take my bow from my hand and carry his bow, my bow, and his backpack for about thirty minutes. That made it easier for me to keep up with him, even though it was still not enough to catch up completely.

Sometimes Jesus takes things from us so we can better follow Him. I have learned that He always allows the backpack to stay on our body to remind us how much we need Him. That backpack truly represents the burdens of life. And no matter how many times He offers to take the burdens away, we find ways to find new ones!

Following Jesus is a test. The test is all about following Him and letting go of the things that are in our hands and the burdens we carry. Jesus tested Philip. He is also testing you and me to see if we are willing to let go of the things of this world so we can keep up with Him. Our goal needs to be to keep up with Jesus. If there is anything at all weighing us down, we need to be willing to let go of those things. We will always carry the pack, but even *that* He offers to carry for us.

Gospel Grit Challenge: Besides your backpack, what is in your hands that is not necessary for the journey? Your exam today is to consider letting go of things in life that are superfluous and not necessary for following Jesus.

T—JOHN 6:43: "DO NOT GRUMBLE AMONG YOURSELVES."

When we are hot, tired, and sweaty, and have no idea how much longer we have to be miserable, we grumble. In this passage, Jesus is telling us not to grumble. He does not have to look back to see grumbling. Jesus hears the grumble like a den of hungry, roaring lions on His heels.

As children, when driving on a long trip my sister and I would often ask our dad the infamous question all children ask: "How much longer?"

As I was out in the woods hunting, on two occasions I finally could not contain myself, and I had to ask the question: "How much longer?" The funny thing was, my friend never would tell me. I must confess I grumbled at times as I thought of how ridiculous our senseless hike was becoming. But the point in backpacking with Jesus is not the destination so much as the journey. Don't get me wrong, the finish line matters, and getting to heaven is paramount. But as you and I travel with Jesus along this path called life, we must remember it is all about following Him, which really translates into being with Him.

Yes, the essence of following Jesus is to be with Him. Who cares where He takes us? Who cares if we do not know where we are going?

Jesus always knows where He is going, and He knows how to lead us. Our task is to follow Him!

Gospel Grit Challenge: Identify any doubts you have about following Jesus. Confess your grumbling and just follow Him!

T—JOHN 6:56: "HE WHO EATS MY FLESH AND DRINKS MY BLOOD ABIDES IN ME, AND I IN HIM."

The centerpiece of the gospel is Jesus Christ. The centerpiece of Jesus Christ is redemption. Redemption leads to relationship. Jesus invites us to follow Him so closely that we are indeed one with Him in relationship. The purpose in following Him is to know Him. To know Him is to abide in Him. But it does not stop there. This verse teaches that He, in return, will abide in us. This verse exposes the heart of the gospel: relationship.

Jesus came for two purposes: first, to satisfy the price for sin; and second, to restore a broken relationship.

After a long day of hunting in the woods, I cannot express to you how good it felt to be back in camp enjoying my humble little tent. I took off my backpack, the one that was filled to the brim with stuff I ended up not needing, took my shoes off, and lay down on my sleeping bag suspended about fourteen inches off the ground on a cot that made me feel as if I were at the Hilton.

I stared at my backpack, reflected on the long hike I had just been on, and before I knew it was sound asleep on my sleeping bag. I was comfortable. I was secure. I was safe. I was in my temporary Hilton for the night. I was no longer stressing out over the hike. I was no longer carrying my backpack. I finally had an opportunity to truly rest my aching bones.

This is a picture of relaxing in Jesus in a relationship that allows us to rest in Him. Jesus asks us to spend some long days out on the trails of life. But there is always that portion of time when He tells us to take off our shoes and rest in Him. In Him we are safe and secure, and the weight of the world seems to be finally off us and on Him. A covenant relationship with Jesus comes when we follow closely behind Him. At our point of exhaustion, Jesus stops for the night and shows us that following Him for the day is worth the discomfort that comes in this life.

We are told that together, we abide in and with one another. What a privilege to abide in Jesus Christ and He in me!

Gospel Grit Challenge: Stop and rest! We live in a fast-paced culture demanding much from us. There must be that moment in your day when you rest in Jesus. Have you taken time to enjoy your relationship with Him today? How?

S—JOHN 6:61: JESUS KNEW THAT HIS DISCIPLES GRUMBLED AT WHAT HE SAID.

This observation is the single most revealing verse in the Gospels on the nature of following Jesus. We would all admit the disciples Jesus picked turned out to be famous, each one in his own right. But during those three years with the homeless God, they had their moments.

Imagine being guilty of grumbling back at God. Wait a minute—we *are* guilty of that! When you are tired and hungry and homeless and carrying a bunch of weight in that old, soiled backpack, you don't always put on a happy face. In fact, life can be really tough some days even if you are following Jesus—*especially* if you are following Jesus. Hang in there. Do not give up.

Winston Churchill is famous for many things, including his speeches. Among his most famous was his shortest, which comprised only seven words. He said, *"Never, never, never, never, never give up!"*

When we catch ourselves grumbling at following Jesus, we need to have in mind that giving up is not an option. No matter how steep the hill He has us climbing, no matter how muddy the swamp He has us wading through, He knows what He is doing, and ours is to follow Him.

Once in a while I truly wonder why God does what God does. I think there are other options that seem far better solutions. Yet God is God, and I am not. Ours is to trust and obey Him. Perhaps we would be wise to open the zipper on our backpack and look in the special little pocket down in the corner where we have housed grumbling. I am certain Jesus would take it from you if you would just give it to Him. Grumbling always affects attitude. Attitude always affects altitude. In order to soar above the swamp, we must get rid of the dead weight called grumbling.

Gospel Grit Challenge: List the complaints you have because you are following Jesus. Looking at your list: has grumbling helped or hurt? Which complaints are you willing to get rid of right now? Do it!

T—JOHN 6:63: "IT IS THE SPIRIT WHO GIVES LIFE; THE FLESH PROFITS NOTHING; THE WORDS THAT I HAVE SPOKEN TO YOU ARE SPIRIT AND ARE LIFE."

Jesus is always taking things and turning them upside down and inside out. For example, He tells us that if we want to be first, then we need to be last. He tells us if we want to be great, we need to be the least. He tells us if we want to be rich, we need to give it all away. These are examples of Jesus taking worldly thinking and turning it on its head. As long as we carry our backpack, Jesus is forever rearranging what we have inside of it. What was important to us is no longer important to us. That is what happens when we follow Jesus.

Now Jesus tells us that what we do in the flesh isn't worth even a cheap backpack. He tells us that words are critically important. He tells us of the importance of living in the spirit. He is rearranging our world. He is rearranging the things in our backpack. Jesus is preparing us for something far greater. Jesus is attempting to pry our backpacks from our lives to make room for something He had in mind all along for each of us. Jesus is preparing you and me to carry His cross.

Yes, the purpose of following Jesus is ultimately to carry His cross.

This is the ultimate in following Jesus. He has hand-tailored His cross to fit your life. All the lessons along the way, all the arranging and rearranging of things in the backpack, were in preparation for the metamorphosis Jesus is about to birth in His followers. We remain in our cocoon until that moment when Jesus sets us free. The irony is we are never free until we carry His cross! This is the essence of following Jesus.

We spend a life outside of Jesus Christ filling our backpack with things from this world that at the time seem really important and necessary. The essence of following Jesus all the way to the end is to empty the backpack so about the only thing there is room for is His cross! This is what is meant by following Jesus. It's getting the world out of us and getting Jesus in us!

> *Gospel Grit Challenge: How close are you to abandoning your backpack and turning it in for His cross? What still has a grip on your life that holds you back from being all God wants you to be? His cross is waiting for you. It is in embracing it that you will be totally free!*

S—JOHN 6:64: JESUS KNEW FROM THE BEGINNING WHO THEY WERE WHO DID NOT BELIEVE, AS WELL AS WHO IT WAS THAT WOULD BETRAY HIM.

There are many things I like about following Jesus: One, He knows what He is doing. Two, He knows where He is going. Three, He knows His audience.

It is critically important for a speaker to connect with his or her audience. If the speaker fails to connect, he or she fails to deliver the message. There are many ways to connect with a message. God chose to connect with us through His Son, Jesus Christ. He chose to have Him wander with purpose through the back roads of Israel for three years to accomplish His plan for mankind. It worked! However, in every crowd there will be naysayers. Jesus certainly had His share. They simply were not willing to buy into His offer. Had Jesus been rich and dressed in the fine linens of the day, it would not have made any difference. It was never about what was on His outer person that caused so many to hate Him. It was *who* He was that caused them to hate Him.

In person as in the first century, or by His Spirit as in the twenty-first century, there are those who will follow Jesus and those who will hate Jesus. Jesus understands. We live in a world filled with betrayals. Many of us have seen our Savior betrayed by people from all walks of life. Our privilege is to follow Jesus no matter what the world decides to do.

Gospel Grit Challenge: Is Jesus enough for you? Who else would you follow if not Jesus?

> T—JOHN 6:65: "NO ONE CAN COME TO ME UNLESS IT HAS BEEN GRANTED HIM FROM THE FATHER."

I got my first GPS as a gift from my daughter for my birthday several years ago. I have a reputation for getting lost the moment I leave my driveway. I have no sense of direction except in New York City.

On my infamous hunting trip, my friend gave me a GPS for the woods. He spent time trying to show me how to use the dumb thing. It was dumb because I never figured out how to use it (except the walkie-talkie part of it).

My friend told me I could be anywhere in the woods and that instrument could get me out. It is important for us to understand that while Jesus was confined to humanity, He had a heavenly Global Positioning System! This verse teaches us that Jesus was being guided by His heavenly Father. How awesome is that?

Who is calling the shots in this world? God Almighty is calling the shots. God is sovereign and all-knowing and ever-present and all-powerful. Yet He cares about giving His Son specific instructions for each of His followers. Truly, He is an amazing God!

When I was in the woods, fighting for my life as it seemed on my hunting trip, food was a high priority. Early in the morning I packed some food that at home I would not be too excited to eat. But in the woods, under the conditions I have been describing, even the simplest of foods seemed like prime rib!

It has always been my practice to pray before I eat, as I am truly grateful to God for the food provided for me. On that day in the woods, my prayer went far beyond giving thanks for what I was about to eat. I gave thanks to God for safety and strength, for my family, for my salvation, and for my future with Jesus in heaven. When you are on the trails of life, away from the normal day-to-day cares, you take time to reflect on things otherwise taken for granted. On that day I took time to thank God for guiding my life and directing me to Himself. Jesus makes it clear to each of us who follow Him that His Father, our Father, is watching and leading and guiding and directing our lives. Praise God!

Gospel Grit Challenge: Find a place in your life today where you can gain an eternal perspective on life. You will discover the greatness of God and will express the deepest appreciation to Him for calling you to follow His Son!

T—JOHN 7:24: "DO NOT JUDGE ACCORDING TO APPEARANCE, BUT JUDGE WITH RIGHTEOUS JUDGMENT."

One reason I've chosen to describe Jesus as homeless and unemployed so often in this book is that He really was. I've also focused on these realities because of where we are in our history and culture in the United States. Unemployment continues to be a major theme for politicians from both parties. So to think of Jesus Christ as unemployed resonates with our culture in our day.

I have talked a lot about homelessness in regard to Jesus, because in our culture we have a bias against those who are homeless. We often think they are lazy, criminal, uneducated, or simply unable to get their act together. We stereotype the homeless. It is difficult to think of God the Son as homeless. It has bothered me every time I have referenced His homelessness. There is something wrong with the idea that a God who came from the riches of heaven would live on earth without anything that could have made life more desirable. Isn't there? This is my guilty conscience at work within me.

I've used the concept of a backpack, even though in the first century Jesus probably carried something more like a sack, because nearly every child in America up to every college student uses a backpack. Many people in business use them too. I use a backpack every day going to work. I exchange my suitcases for backpacks when I travel. To think Jesus Christ had little more than a backpack creates even more guilt for me as I continue to accumulate riches for myself in this life.

Jesus is calling us to a life of simplicity. He tells us not to judge others. He tells us that we have no idea the story of the homeless, the unemployed, the poor, and the downtrodden. He is telling us to see people the way He does. An important part of following Jesus is to think the way Jesus thinks. This includes how we think about people.

If we can grasp the truth that none of us are worthy of His high calling, that none of us are righteous and that we are all the same at the foot of the cross, then there will be nothing in this world that hinders our loving view of people.

Gospel Grit Challenge: Have you ever misjudged someone? Who could you benefit from by sitting down with them and asking them to tell their story to you? Pick someone who is not like you and try it out!

S—JOHN 8:59: THEY PICKED UP STONES TO THROW AT HIM, BUT JESUS HID HIMSELF AND WENT OUT OF THE TEMPLE.

Murder! When we see this picture of hatred, we must take it for what it was: an attempt at murder. There were people who hated Jesus so much all they could think about was how to kill Him. Imagine being created by God only to become the one who would kill the Son of

God! I wouldn't want that one on me.

As His followers, Jesus tells us that people are going to hate us too! That kind of persecution hasn't come to us yet in full force, but it is on its way. Hatred toward followers of Jesus Christ in the United States of America is coming to a town near you.

When I began pastoral ministry over thirty years ago, I felt I was in the majority in this country as far as what I believed and who I believed in and what I stood for. Today, I absolutely believe I am in the minority in every category. Times are rapidly changing. We must take following Jesus seriously because we live in serious times.

In each of our backpacks, we must find a large dose of gospel grit! It is going to take our best to withstand what is coming our way. We must recognize the times in which we live and realize it is no longer business as usual. Following Christ for us in the United States must become what it has been for followers in countries where persecution is common.

Following Jesus not to gain health and wealth but to endure sorrow and suffering is a game changer. I trust you are still willing to follow Him. Following Jesus during the best of times is easy. Following Jesus during the worst of times is going to be exciting and very rewarding. Hang in there and keep following!

Gospel Grit Challenge: Identify ways Christianity has changed in your lifetime in the United States. Describe the state of Christianity in the United States ten years from now!

T—JOHN 14:1: "DO NOT LET YOUR HEART BE TROUBLED; BELIEVE IN GOD, BELIEVE ALSO IN ME."

JUST DO IT!

Gospel Grit Challenge: Just do it!

> T—JOHN 14:12: "HE WHO BELIEVES IN ME, THE WORKS THAT I DO, HE WILL DO ALSO; AND GREATER WORKS THAN THESE HE WILL DO; BECAUSE I GO TO THE FATHER."

As I reflect on my recent hunting trip, I decide to give up on my friend's type of bow hunting, as I will never be as strong or fast or skilled in the woods as he is. But when next bow season comes around, I know I will give it another try!

Read the verse above again. I am amazed that Jesus would make such a bold statement to us after almost three years with Him. After all the garbage we have hauled with us for three years, He is telling us that we are going to do *greater* things than He did! This does not seem likely in the flesh. But that's the point: following Jesus is not to be done in the flesh! He asks us to follow Him in such a way that we can carry on His ministry for our generation.

The things in our backpacks change because our hearts change. Our hearts become transformed when we follow Jesus. We become a miracle in the making, a work in progress. All the time we are focusing on that silly backpack, Jesus is focusing on our hearts.

Have you noticed that once you give your heart to someone or something, you give 100 percent? I gave my wife my heart over thirty-one years ago, and the reason it cannot go anywhere else is that she keeps it in the vault of her heart. Jesus has a very large vault. His desire is to place your heart in His vault for safekeeping! Your life will be filled with joy, you will bear much fruit, and you will find ultimate purpose and meaning for your life if you give Jesus *all* your heart. It really is that simple!

Gospel Grit Challenge: Does God have your heart? If He has your money, your time, your priorities, your dreams, and your love, then make no mistake: He has your heart in His vault for safekeeping!

> T—JOHN 15:2: "EVERY BRANCH IN ME THAT DOES NOT BEAR FRUIT,
> HE TAKES AWAY; AND EVERY BRANCH THAT BEARS FRUIT, HE PRUNES IT
> SO THAT IT MAY BEAR MORE FRUIT."

Christianity is all about reproduction! The fruit of following Jesus is producing others who will follow Jesus. Following Jesus in not only about what is in your backpack, but about helping others empty their backpacks through your example. Consider yourself a trailblazer for God.

I grew up in the greater Portland, Oregon area. We have an NBA team called the Portland Trailblazers. There were some great years when they lived up to their name. But most of their franchise history has been a disappointment. In the 1976–77 season, we won the title. Blazer mania was born! Wouldn't it be great for us as His followers to create a little Jesus mania? All it takes is following Him with your whole heart. May God grant us the courage to be part of something bigger than ourselves. God, may You grant our generation the birth of Jesus mania!

Gospel Grit Challenge: Are you all-in yet? Think of the lives that will thank you in heaven because you were all-in for Jesus!

> T—JOHN 15:4–5: "ABIDE IN ME, AND I IN YOU…APART FROM ME YOU
> CAN DO NOTHING."

(See also John 15:6; two references.)

How many times have we taken off without Jesus? That is exactly what He does not want us to do. Many people are talented and gifted and experienced, so why follow Jesus?

This becomes the challenge within Christianity. Is it true we cannot do anything without Him? Are there things we can do without Him? After all, we do things all the time without His help. *But that's the problem!* The things we do are always in the flesh. The things He does *through* us are always done in the spirit. This is why the main focus of following Him is abiding in Him. We can't do this on our own.

At times, we seem to have just enough goodies in our backpacks to leave Jesus out of the picture. I call these goodies artificial props because they are just that, artificial. I like quality stuff when I can afford it. I have not yet described to you the backpack I use from day to day: It is a camel-brown law enforcement backpack that is the most awesome backpack I have ever owned. It has more zippers than stars in the sky. It has more pockets than a clown's costume. It has more features than a stealth bomber. Add them all up, and that backpack can be a replacement for my need for Jesus. *That's the problem.* Now you know why Jesus ultimately wants to get our backpacks from us! As long as we have a crutch, we don't see the urgency to include Jesus in our plans. If we could just get it through our heads that without Jesus we can do nothing that will last, we would be the better for it.

Gospel Grit Challenge: Make it a practice to ask God for help before doing anything at all. When something is completed, make a point to thank God for His help and then give Him all the glory for anything you may have accomplished!

T—JOHN 15:16: "I CHOSE YOU, AND APPOINTED YOU THAT YOU WOULD GO AND BEAR FRUIT."

We have talked about bearing fruit. We have talked about following Jesus. We need to spend a few moments on being chosen for the team.

As a grade-school boy, I was on the small side of the scale. In sixth grade I was short and husky. I will never forget a September afternoon during PE when we were to play a game of flag football. The PE teacher chose two captains, and they began choosing their teams. You guessed it. I was the last one picked. I was humiliated and embarrassed. I will never forget that day.

If you are following Jesus, you have been picked, and not because there were no other options. You were picked because God has an assignment for you. Your primary assignment is to follow Jesus and wait until further instructions are given to you. You follow Him by being in the Word and in prayer daily and by obeying what He tells you to do. Your assignment is to be like Jesus.

On days when you do not feel like putting on your backpack and following Jesus, I would remind you it is not about you! It is all about Him. He is the coach; He is calling the plays. Our assignment is to execute the play. It really does not matter if we like the play or not. It really does not matter if we think the play will work or not. We are not in charge! God is in charge. That is the nature of following Jesus, and it is the hardest part about following Him. Control is the giant many of us are still trying to carry in our backpacks. But if you're going to get anywhere, you've got to let it go.

Gospel Grit Challenge: If you are willing to make them your passion, write in your Bible the following phrases: "I am a lifer for God. I will follow Jesus no matter what."

T—JOHN 15:23: "HE WHO HATES ME HATES MY FATHER ALSO."

Before Jesus finishes His three years with us, He wants to make sure there are a few things we understand and never forget. Jesus is always connecting Himself to His Father. This is a good thing, because His connection connects *us* to the God of the universe.

Jesus wants us to always remember that as He and His Father are one, so we are to be one with Him. As we are one with Him, we become one with His Father, our heavenly Father. What a privilege! This ought to be the only reason needed to follow Jesus closely every day no matter what!

Hate is a strong word in any culture. It represents and conveys a strong message. As His followers, we simply need to be reminded that there will be people who will always hate Jesus.

Several weeks ago I watched the Democratic Convention at a moment when they were voting on the inclusion or exclusion of God in their party platform. I will never forget the man the cameras zoomed in on who violently waved his arms in opposition to including God. The chairman called for a vote three times, because he knew the delegates were voting in a way he had been instructed to rule against. Clearly, the delegates did not vote to include God, yet the chair ruled according to what had already been written on the teleprompter.

Each person votes in this life, and each person must stand before God on judgment day. I have chosen to follow Jesus all the way. I trust you will join me!

Gospel Grit Challenge: How will you handle those who hate God? How will you act on your privilege of becoming one with the Father?

T—JOHN 15:27: "YOU WILL TESTIFY ALSO, BECAUSE YOU HAVE BEEN WITH ME FROM THE BEGINNING."

It's incredibly rewarding to be in on something from the ground floor and later see what has been accomplished. That is the sort of satisfaction you will have if you follow Jesus closely all the way. It should be our goal to be with Jesus "from the beginning."

The number-one song of the twentieth century was by the Rolling Stones: "I Can't Get No Satisfaction." I love the lyrics because they so represent our efforts outside of Jesus Christ. When I find something I like, I stick with it. I have been eating at the same hot-dog stand in Jennings Lodge since I was a little boy. I have had the same wife for thirty-one years. I own one suit and wear it every Sunday until it wears out, and then I buy another one and do it all over again. I have the same golf bag I had when I got married. I have the same Bible cover I had when I was in college. I am just that sort of a guy. And I have had the same God since age seven.

Our testimony is the most powerful weapon we possess as followers of Jesus Christ. It is the story of our journey with Jesus. It is the story of the days we followed Him closely and the days we did not. Your backpack, too, is part of your testimony. Hopefully, as the years roll by, that old backpack becomes a memorial to what God has done along the way.

I am certain you have underestimated the power of your personal testimony. Your Gospel Grit Challenge will take quite a bit of time, but it will be well worth it to articulate your story.

Gospel Grit Challenge: Write out a thirty-second testimony, a two-minute testimony, and a five-minute testimony for yourself. Spend the majority of your time talking about life after meeting Jesus rather than life before meeting Jesus.

> T—JOHN 16:20: "YOU WILL WEEP AND LAMENT, BUT THE WORLD WILL REJOICE; YOU WILL GRIEVE, BUT YOUR GRIEF WILL BE TURNED INTO JOY."

Before we set out on our hunting trip, my friend talked me into buying a special permit that gave us permission to hunt on some government land that was legal by permit only. It turns out we were the only two hunters who purchased the tags, and therefore we had an entire unit to ourselves! That is very rare in the state of Oregon. Perhaps that is why we saw elk both morning and evening.

I balked at buying the tag at first because it was so expensive. My friend convinced me it was worth the price of admission. It turned out he was right—again.

Jesus has asked us to buy a special tag that allows us to follow Him where few people have trodden before. We look at the cost factor and recognize there is a high price to pay when we follow after Jesus Christ. Just when we think the cost is too high, Jesus reminds us of the rewards of following Him. Those of us following Him have paid for the special tag. Is it worth it? If you have to ask that question, you did not buy the same tag I did. Of course it is worth it!

I have gone through heartache as a child and as an adult. The death of my son was about as bad as it gets. But I never stop following Jesus, even when I think He could have done me one better with my son! He is waiting for me at the finish. The goal in following Jesus is to stay with Him all the way until we cross the finish line. On that day, at that moment, we will cross over a mountain of backpacks to the other side, and we will finally be reunited with our loved ones and ultimately with Jesus. Oh yes, it is worth the price of admission to follow Jesus!

Gospel Grit Challenge: Memorize this quote from Bill Borden, a missionary who died as a young man while on his mission field. This was found written in his Bible: "No Reserve, No Retreat, And No Regret. Outside a faith in Christ, there is no explanation for such a life."

T: JOHN 21:15: "TEND MY LAMBS."

Sheep follow. People follow. If people aren't following Jesus, they are following someone else. We, His followers, have been given the enormous task to care for other followers of Jesus Christ. It is imperative we get this right because there is so much on the line.

There are many things in life that, when you boil it all down, do not matter. Sports are a great example of that. At the moment, the game seems to be the most important event in life. One year later, one decade later, does anybody remember the average game? Do we actually remember who won, much less who lost? Is there any way we know who lost in the pennant race, much less the World Series?

When it comes to souls, we are talking about things that are eternal. The things that are eternal are the things that should matter most in life. Therefore, people are the ones that matter most.

The reason why the backpack image is so important is because it contains within it elements of the eternal. The choices we make with the things in that backpack really matter. Our responsibility is to help people make right decisions with their backpacks and what they carry in them, and ultimately to trade their backpacks in for the cross. Helping them in this way is what it means to take care of people. The greatest things we are freed from are the cares of this world. We are freed from the cares of surviving, and in Christ we can really live!

Gospel Grit Challenge: List the people you need to tend to in the kingdom of God. Who can you mentor? Who are you influencing? Who do you think is watching you? Who is in need of your help today? Tend His sheep!

S—JOHN 21:25: THERE ARE MANY OTHER THINGS THAT JESUS DID, WHICH IF THEY WERE WRITTEN IN DETAIL, EVEN THE WORLD ITSELF COULD NOT CONTAIN THE BOOKS THAT WOULD BE WRITTEN.

With this verse, we're done—but no, we aren't. Following Jesus is never a start-and-stop proposition. This verse is the conclusion of following Jesus in the Gospels, and it tells us there is no conclusion. There is a beginning but no end. This is the nature of things that are eternal.

In the writings of Matthew, Mark, Luke, and John, we have a brief sketch of what it was like to backpack with Jesus through the mountains and valleys of Israel. This verse tells us there is much more to His story. We will have to wait until heaven to have Him fill us in on all the exciting adventures awaiting us.

At the same time, as His followers from around the world gather together at His feet and as generations come together from all walks of life, as the throng of God's people gathers together, perhaps we will share stories with one another describing the amazing places we were able to travel with Jesus. We will humbly, joyfully gather in His presence and begin to praise Him for all eternity. *Hallelujah, what a Savior!*

Gospel Grit Challenge: Follow Jesus!

SCRIPTURES FROM THE GOSPEL OF JOHN FOR FURTHER STUDY

581. S—John 1:12: But as many as received Him, to them He gave the right to become the children of God, even to those who believe in His name.

582. S—John 1:14: And the Word became flesh, and dwelt among us, and we saw His glory, glory as of the only begotten from the Father, full of grace and truth.

583. T—John 1:43: To Philip: "Follow Me."

584. S—John 2:1–11: Turning water to wine was the beginning of the signs Jesus did in Cana of Galilee to manifest His glory; and His disciples believed in Him.

585. S—John 2:15: He made a scourge of cords, and drove the money changers out of the temple, with the sheep and the oxen that were being sold; and He poured out the coins of the money changers and overturned their table.

586. T—John 2:16: "Take these things away; stop making My Father's house a place of business."

587. S—John 2:23: Many believed as they observed the signs Jesus was doing.

588. S—John 2:24: For His part, Jesus did not entrust Himself to them, for He knew all men.

589. T—John 3:3: "Unless one is born again he cannot see the kingdom of God."

590. T—John 3:5: "Unless one is born of water and the Spirit, he cannot enter into the kingdom of God."

591. T—John 3:7: "Do not be amazed that I said to you, 'You must be born again.'"

592. T—John 3:15: "Whoever believes in Him will have eternal life."

593. T—John 3:16: "Whoever believes in Him shall not perish, but have eternal life."

594. T—John 3:18: "He who believes in Him is not judged; he who does not believe has been judged already."

595. T—John 3:21: "But he who practices the truth comes to the Light, so that his deeds may be manifested as having been wrought in God."

596. S—John 3:22: He spent time with the disciples and baptizing.

597. S—John 4:2: Although Jesus Himself was not baptizing, His disciples were.

598. S—John 4:6: Jesus, weary from His journey, sat down by the well.

599. T—John 4:7: "Give me a drink."

600. T—John 4:13: "Everyone who drinks of this water will thirst again."

601. T—John 4:14: "Whoever drinks of the water that I will give him shall never thirst."

602. T—John 4:24: "God is spirit, and those who worship Him must worship in spirit and truth."

603. T—John 4:32: "I have food to eat that you do not know about."

604. S—John 4:41: Many more believed because of what Jesus said.

605. T—John 4:48: "Unless you people see signs and wonders, you simply will not believe."

606. S—John 4:50: Jesus heals a father's son.

607. S—John 4:54: Jesus performed a second sign after He came out of Judea into Galilee.

608. S—John 5:5–6: When Jesus saw the man lying by the pool of Bethesda, He knew that he had been in that condition for a long time.

609. S—John 5:8: Jesus healed a man who had been sick for thirty-eight years.

610. S—John 5:13: Jesus slipped away in the crowd.

611. T—John 5:14: "Do not sin anymore, so that nothing worse happens to you."

612. T—John 5:24: "He who hears My word, and believes Him who sent Me, has eternal life, and does not come into judgment, but has passed out of death unto life."

613. T—John 5:38: "You do not have His word abiding in you, for you do not believe Him whom He sent."

614. T—John 5:39: "You search the Scriptures because you think that in them you have eternal life."

615. T—John 5:40: "And you are unwilling to come to Me so that you may have life."

616. T—John 5:46–47: "For if you believe Moses, you would believe Me, for he wrote about Me. But if you do not believe his writings, how will you believe My words?"

617. S—John 6:3: Jesus went up on the mountain and sat there with His disciples.

618. S—John 6:5: Jesus saw a large crowd coming to Him.

619. S—John 6:6: He tested Philip; He knew what he intended to do.

620. S—John 6:11: After giving thanks for the bread, Jesus distributed it to those who were seated and did likewise with the fish, giving the people as much as they wanted.

621. T—John 6:12: "Gather up the leftover fragments that nothing will be lost."

622. S—John 6:15: Jesus perceived their intention to come and take Him by force to make Him king; He withdrew again to be alone.

623. S—John 6:19: The disciples saw Jesus walking on the sea.

624. T—John 6:20: "It is I; do not be afraid."

625. T—John 6:27: "Do not work for the food which perishes, but for the food which endures to eternal life."

626. T—John 6:29: "This is the work of God, that you believe in Him whom He has sent."

627. T—John 6:35: "He who believes in Me will never thirst."

628. T—John 6:43: "Do not grumble among yourselves."

629. T—John 6:47: "He who believes has eternal life."

630. T—John 6:51: "I am the living bread that came down out of Heaven; if anyone eats of this bread, he will live forever."

631. T —John 6:53–54: "Unless you eat the flesh of the Son of Man and drink His blood, you have no life in yourselves. He who eats

My flesh and drinks My blood has eternal life, and I will raise him up on the last day."

632. T—John 6:56: "He who eats My flesh and drinks My blood abides in Me, and I in him."

633. T—John 6:58: "He who eats this bread will live forever."

634. S—John 6:59: He taught in the synagogues in Capernaum.

635. S—John 6:61: Jesus knew that His disciples grumbled at what He said.

636. T—John 6:63: "It is the spirit who gives life; the flesh profits nothing; the words that I have spoken to you are spirit and are life."

637. S—John 6:64: Jesus knew from the beginning who they were who did not believe, as well as who it was that would betray Him.

638. T—John 6:65: "No one can come to Me unless it has been granted him from the Father."

639. S—John 7:1: After these things, Jesus walked in Galilee (and not in Judea) because the Jews were seeking to kill Him.

640. S—John 7:10: He went up to the feast, but not publicly.

641. S—John 7:14: In the midst of the feast, Jesus went up into the temple and began to teach.

642. T—John 7:24: "Do not judge according to appearance, but judge with righteous judgment."

643. T—John 7:37–38: "If anyone is thirsty, let him come to Me and drink. He who believes in Me, as the Scripture said, 'From his innermost being will flow rivers of living water."

644. S—John 8:2: Early in the morning, He came again into the temple, and all the people came to Him; He sat down and taught them.

645. S—John 8:6: Jesus stooped down, and wrote on the ground with His finger.

646. T—John 8:7: "He who is without sin among you, let him be the first to throw a stone at her."

647. S—John 8:8: Again He stooped down and wrote on the ground.

648. T—John 8:11: "I do not condemn you either. Go. From now on sin no more."

649. T—John 8:12: "He who follows Me will not walk in the darkness, but will have the Light of life."

650. T—John 8:19: "If you knew Me, you would know My Father also."

651. S—John 8:20: He taught in the temple.

652. T—John 8:24: "Unless you believe that I am He, you will die in your sins."

653. S—John 8:30: He spoke, and many came to believe in Him.

654. T—John 8:31–32: "If you continue in My word, then you are truly disciples of Mine; and you will know the truth, and the truth will make you free."

655. T—John 8:47: "He who is of God hears the words of God; for this reason you do not hear them, because you are not of God."

656. T—John 8:51: "If anyone keeps My word he will never see death."

657. S—John 8:59: They picked up stones to throw at Him, but Jesus hid Himself and went out of the temple.

658. S—John 9:1: As He passed by him, Jesus saw a man who had been blind from birth.

659. S—John 9:6: He spit on the ground and made clay of the spittle, then applied the clay to the blind man's eyes.

660. T—John 10:9: "I am the door; if anyone enters through Me, he will be saved, and will go in and out and find pasture."

661. T—John 10:27: "My sheep hear My voice, and I know them, and they follow Me."

662. S—John 11:3: The disciples, speaking of Lazarus: "He whom You love is sick."

663. S—John 11:5: Jesus loved Martha and her sister Mary and their brother Lazarus.

664. T—John 11:25: "He who believes in Me will live even if he dies."

665. S—John 11:33: Mary wept; Jesus was deeply moved in spirit and was troubled.

666. S—John 11:35: Jesus wept.

667. S—John 11:38: Jesus was deeply moved within.

668. S—John 11:43–44: Jesus raised Lazarus from the dead.

669. S—John 11:54: Jesus therefore no longer continued to walk publicly among the Jews, but He went away from there to the country near the wilderness into a city called Ephraim and stayed there with the disciples.

670. T—John 12:8: "You always have the poor with you, but do not always have Me."

671. T—John 12:24–26: "Unless a grain of wheat falls into the earth and dies, it remains alone; but if it dies, it bears much fruit. He who loves his life loses it, and he who hates his life in this world will keep it to life eternal. If anyone serves Me, he must follow Me; and where I am, there My servant will be also; if anyone serves Me, the Father will honor him."

672. T—John 12:35–36: "Walk while you have the Light, so that darkness will not overtake you; he who walks in the darkness does not know where he goes. While you have the Light, believe in the Light, so that you may become sons of Light."

673. S—John 12:36: Jesus departed and hid Himself from them.

674. T—John 12:44: "He who believes in Me, does not believe in Me but in Him who sent Me."

675. T—John 12:46: "That everyone who believes in Me will not remain in darkness."

676. T—John 12:48: "He who rejects Me and does not receive My sayings, has one who judges him; the word I spoke is what will judge him at the last day."

677. S—John 13:1: Having loved His own who were in the world, He loved them to the end.

678. S—John 13:5: Jesus washed the disciples' feet.

679. T—John 13:8: "If I do not wash you, you have no part with Me."

680. S—John 13:11: He knew the one who was betraying Him.

681. T—John 13:15: "For I gave you an example that you also should do as I did to you."

682. T—John 13:34–35: "A new commandment I give to you, that you love one another, even as I have loved you, that you also love one another. By this all men will know that you are My disciples, if

you have love for one another."

683. T—John 14:1: "Do not let your heart be troubled; believe in God, believe also in Me."

684. T—John 14:12: "He who believes in Me, the works that I do, he will do also; and greater works than these he will do; because I go to the Father."

685. T—John 14:13–15: "And whatever you ask in My name, that will I do, so that the Father may be glorified in the Son. If you ask Me anything in My name, I will do it. If you love Me, you will keep My commandments."

686. T—John 14:21: "He who has my commandments and keeps them is the one who loves Me; and he who loves Me will be loved by My Father, and I will love him and will disclose Myself to him."

687. T—John 14:23: "If anyone loves Me, he will keep My word."

688. T—John 14:27: "Do not let your heart be troubled, nor let it be fearful."

689. T—John 15:2: "Every branch in Me that does not bear fruit, He takes away; and every branch that bears fruit, He prunes it so that it may bear more fruit."

690. T—John 15:4–5: "Abide in Me, and I in you…apart from Me you can do nothing."

691. T—John 15:6: "If anyone does not abide in Me, he is thrown away as a branch and dries up."

692. T—John 15:7: "If you abide in Me, and My words abide in you, ask whatever you wish, and it will be done for you."

693. T—John 15:9: "Abide in My love."

694. T—John 15:10: "If you keep My commandments, you will abide in My love."

695. T—John 15:12: "This is My commandment, that you love one another, just as I have loved you."

696. T—John 15:14: "You are My friends if you do what I command you."

697. T—John 15:16: "I chose you, and appointed you that you would go and bear fruit."

698. T—John 15:17: "This I command you, that you love one another."

699. T—John 15:23: "He who hates Me hates My Father also."

700. T—John 15:27: "You will testify also, because you have been with Me from the beginning."

701. T—John 16:20: "You will weep and lament, but the world will rejoice; you will grieve, but your grief will be turned into joy."

702. T—John 16:24: "Ask and you will receive, so that your joy may be made full."

703. T—John 16:33: "In the world you have tribulation, but take courage; I have overcome the world."

704. T—John 17:1: "Jesus spoke, lifted His eyes to Heaven, and said, 'Father, the hour has come; glorify Your Son, that the Son may glorify You.'"

705. T—John 17:2–26: Jesus prayed many specific prayers for His disciples.

706. S—John 18:4: Jesus knew all the things that were coming on Him.

707. T—John 18:11: When Peter cut off Malchus's ear: "Put the sword into the sheath."

708. S—John 19:1: Pilate took Jesus and scourged Him.

709. T—John 19:28: "I am thirsty."

710. S—John 19:30: He bowed His head and gave up His spirit.

711. S—John 19:34: One of the soldiers pierced His side with a spear, and immediately blood and water came out.

712. T—John 20:17: "Stop clinging to Me, for I have not yet ascended to the Father; but go to My brethren, and say to them, 'I ascend to My Father and your Father, and My God and your God.'"

713. S—John 20:19: Jesus came and stood in their midst.

714. T—John 20:19: "Peace be with you."

715. T—John 20:21: "Peace be with you; as the Father has sent Me, I also send you."

716. T—John 20:22: "Receive the Holy Spirit."

717. T—John 20:23: "If you forgive the sins of any, their sins have been forgiven them; if you retain the sins of any, they have been retained."

718. T—John 20:26: "Peace be with you."
719. T—John 20:29: "Blessed are they who did not see, and yet believed."
720. S—John 20:30–31: In the presence of His disciples, Jesus performed many other signs, which are not written in this book; but these have been written so you may believe that Jesus is the Christ, the Son of God, and that believing you may have life in His name.
721. S—John 21:1: After these things, Jesus manifested Himself again to the disciples.
722. T—John 21:6: "Cast the net on the right-hand side of the boat and you will find a catch."
723. T—John 21:10: "Bring some of the fish which you have now caught."
724. T—John 21:12: "Come and have breakfast."
725. T—John 21:15: "Tend My lambs."
726. T—John 21:16: "Tend My sheep."
727. T—John 21:17: "Tend My sheep."
728. T—John 21:19: "Follow Me!"
729. S—John 21:25: There are many other things that Jesus did, which if they were written in detail, even the world itself could not contain the books that would be written.

No matter what happens today, God loves you very much!

AFTERWORD:
COMMENTS ON HEAVEN AND HELL

I believe in a literal heaven and a literal hell. I believe the Bible clearly teaches them. Ten years ago I became acquainted with the writings of Randy Alcorn, whom I consider to be the premier authority on the subject of heaven. I have read all his material on heaven and beyond.

As I assembled this book, I deliberately left out most passages referencing both heaven and hell. I left them out not because they are not true or because they do not have some influence on my subject matter, but because they stand alone. My subject matter for this book is the "here and now," not the "then and later." In using verses on eternity, I saw the strong potential for getting off the main subject, which is following Jesus on this very day. Verses on eternity tend to make us think about what is to come, and we can lose our focus on the matter at hand—living strong for Jesus today!

Since the homegoing of my son ten years ago, I have become a student of the subject of heaven. Likewise, I have been a student my entire life on the subject of hell. I am currently writing a book on it. I have studied the subject most of my adult life and have taught many classes on hell to both youth and adults. As a child, I was saved by a "hell sermon." I have a strong passion to communicate this subject to those who will read what I write. But again, the focus of *this* book is not the subject of hell. Therefore I have omitted most mentions of it from this text, not because it is not important or true, but because it, like the subject of heaven, would take us away from the thrust of this book, which is living strong for Jesus today!

I would love to stay in touch with you. I have a daily devotional Monday–Thursday you can find at my website. You may also contact me at:

Website: randybutlerbooks.com

E-mail: randy@salemec.com

Or you may contact me through Deep River Books. I would love to hear from you and share in your struggles and your victories.

ACKNOWLEDGMENTS

I want to thank the dear people at Deep River Books for publishing *Gospel Grit*. Their work with me has been nothing short of outstanding. They are a class act!

I want to thank Nancie Carmichael for taking the time to make my manuscript far better than what I first gave her. Likewise, I am indebted to her for the time she gave to writing the foreword to this book. She is a saint!

I want to thank my editor, Rachel Starr Thomson, who also edited my second book. I met her last year at the ICRS conference in Florida, where she agreed to edit my third book, which you have in your hand. She is a young, godly, brilliant woman who filed the rough edges off my jagged manuscript. She deserves a ton of credit!

I want to thank Bruce Robbins, my hunting friend, who became the inspiration for my comments and illustrations on the Gospel of John.

I want to thank God for helping me write this book. He has been so gracious and kind to me. I owe Him all that I have in this life. I love Him with all my heart!

I want to acknowledge my wife, Joanie, who shapes many of my thoughts, and my daughter, Kristi, who means the world to me. How we look forward to the reunion with Kevin when we are together as a family once again in heaven!

OTHER DEEP RIVER BOOKS BY RANDY BUTLER:

ISBN: 978-1935265849

ISBN: 978-1937756123